D0953091

Angels, MIRACLES, and Messages

A Guideposts Book

Angels, MIRACLES, and Messages

A *Guideposts* Book

Publishers Since 1798

THOMAS NELSON PUBLISHERS
Nashville • Atlanta • London • Vancouver
Printed in the United States of America

Every attempt has been made to credit the sources of copyright material used in this book. If any such acknowledgment has been inadvertently omitted or miscredited, receipt of such information would be appreciated.

Published in Nashville, Tennessee, by Thomas Nelson, Inc.

Unless otherwise noted, all Scripture quotations are from the *King James or Authorized Version of the Bible*.

Scripture quotations marked NRSV are from the *New Revised Standard Version of the Bible*, copyright © 1946, 1952, 1971 by the Division of Christian Education of the National Council of Churches of Christ in the U.S.A. and are used by permission.

Scripture quotations marked RSV are from the *Revised Standard Version of the Bible*, copyright 1946, 1952, 1971 by the Division of Christian Education of the National Council of the Churches of Christ in the United States of America and are used by permission.

Scripture quotations marked TLB are from *The Living Bible*, © 1971. Used by permission of Tyndale House Publishers, Inc., Wheaton, IL 60189. All rights reserved.

Except as noted below, and for the poems, all material appeared originally in *Guideposts* magazine. Copyright © 1950, 1968, 1971, 1973, 1974, 1979, 1982, 1983, 1986, 1988, 1989, 1990, 1991, 1992, 1993, 1994, 1995.

"The Invisible Finger" by Daniel Schantz is from *Daily Guideposts, 1993*. Copyright © 1992 by Guideposts, Carmel, NY 10512.

"The Angel of Opportunity" by Fay Angus is from *Daily Guideposts, 1992*. Copyright © 1991 by Guideposts, Carmel, NY 10512.

"The Sign of the Dolphin" by Sue Monk Kidd is from *Daily Guideposts, 1988*. Copyright © 1987 by Guideposts, Carmel, NY 10512.

"The Timeless Moment" by Elaine St. Johns is adapted from *Dawnings*. Copyright © 1981 by Guideposts, Carmel, NY 10512.

"A Stirring to Pray" by E. Ruth Glover. Copyright © 1987 by E. Ruth Glover.

"The Man on the Rock" by Patsy Ruth Miller is adapted from *My Hollywood: When Both of Us Were Young*. Copyright © 1988 by Patsy Ruth Miller.

Library of Congress Cataloging-in-Publication Data

Angels, miracles, and messages.
    p.   cm.
    Collections of stories previously published from *Guideposts* magazine.
    Issue also under title: His Mysterious Ways, Volume IV.
    "A Guideposts Book."
    ISBN 0-7852-7400-6
    1. Meditations. I. Guideposts (Carmel, N.Y.)
BV4832.2.A65 1996
242—dc20
                             95-43761
                             CIP

7 — 02 01 00 99 98
Book design by Monica Elias
Printed in the United States of America

CONTENTS

GOD'S MESSAGES DIRECT US

GOD'S ANGELS HELP US

GOD'S PRESENCE CHANGES US

GOD'S LOVE ASSURES US OF LIFE AFTER DEATH

GOD'S PLAN INCLUDES US

GOD'S WONDERS WORK FOR US

INTRODUCTION

"These books are such treasures," a reader commented of previous collections of stories from *Guideposts* magazine. But, she said, as each one came out, she looked for her favorite story, only to be disappointed. It was the story of Bud Ward who found healing after a stroke when he struggled to photograph a shed on fire—and in the process discovered that one of the slides showed Jesus in the fire.

Well, we have taken the hint and included that story in this volume, along with more than fifty-five others. Perhaps among them you'll find one of your favorites that has never appeared in a previous collection.

Angels, Miracles, and Messages celebrates God's care and concern for us and the surprising ways He directs our lives. He can arrange a whole series of events, involving many people, to bring the answers to our prayers, or He can meet our need through one tiny piece of seed fluff in a mountain wilderness. Sometimes He sends a mysterious stranger to help us, or to challenge us—someone who disappears as soon as the work is done. At other times He uses us in His mysterious ways, so that we become the answer to someone else's need. He continues to speak to us in whispers and dreams, in shouts and intuition. In His planning, there are no coincidences, just the working out of His purposes in ways that often defy explanation.

As you read this new collection, we hope not only that you'll be inspired by the stories, but also that you'll be on the lookout for the mysterious ways in which God works His wonders in your life.

—The Editors of Guideposts

GOD'S PROVIDENCE PREPARES US

You show me the path of life. . . .
—Psalm 16:11 (NRSV)

"Take note, I have told you beforehand."
—Matthew 24:25 (NRSV)

"MAN IN THE WATER!"
— Marilyn Beis —

I rarely went into downtown Chicago, but early one morning in May 1978, while my husband was at work and my two children in school, I decided to go into the city to look up an old newspaper article for a friend. It was about nine o'clock, brisk and chilly, when I headed across the Michigan Avenue Bridge toward the Sun Times Building.

Then something very strange happened. From somewhere inside my head I heard a distinct inner voice crying: "Man in the water! Man in the water!" I leaned over the railing, feeling a bit foolish, and peered into the greenish-brown murk of the Chicago River. There was no one. Nothing but bits of floating garbage and an unappealing film of pollution.

Thank God no one's actually in there, I thought with relief. *I guess I was just daydreaming.* The call I heard sounded like an appeal for help—and I was not the heroic type. I hadn't even gone swimming in years. As a homemaker in suburban Evanston, Illinois, the only exercise I got was taking care of the house and my family. Yet, ever since I had become an active Christian two and a half years ago, I had been concerned about how to relate the parable of the Good Samaritan to my own life. How do we help others, including strangers, in difficult and even dangerous situations? As I continued across the bridge my relief was mixed with dismay at the realization that a man in the water was not something I really felt equal to. *There are policemen, firemen, emergency squads for that kind of thing,* I thought. *I'm just an average person.*

At ten o'clock, my research at the *Sun Times* finished, I walked back over the bridge, the inner call I had heard just an hour earlier forgotten, my mind on other things. Then like a piercing alarm jolting me to attention, I heard almost the same words, but this time unmistakably real and urgent: "Man overboard! Man overboard!" Ahead of me on the bridge, a man was shouting and gesturing wildly, trying to get the attention of two dockmen below.

I ran over to him. "What happened?" I asked.

"He jumped! I saw him—just a few seconds ago."

This time, when I looked over the railing, I saw a frightening and pathetic sight. Thirty feet below, in the river, was a man fully clothed. He was only about ten feet from the dock but he made no effort to save himself. He just lay passively in the water, either unconscious, drugged, or simply willing to die. I felt paralyzed. A feeling of unreality came over me, as if it weren't really happening—as if I were watching footage on the five o'clock news.

At last the two dockmen realized what was happening and flung a life ring into the water. But it did no good.

The rope tangled, and in any case the man was unable to get it.

Now, as I watched in horror, the man slowly began to sink under water. Just as he was almost out of sight one of the dockmen dived in and grasped him by the hair. He pulled him up to the surface but then he seemed to be in trouble himself, gasping and spitting as he called for help. "Someone up there, help me!" he screamed. "I can't hold him up myself!"

The other dockman was frantically attempting to untangle another rope to throw in from the dock. On the bridge a fascinated audience of about one hundred passersby watched—but no one moved.

The thought came to me—*Could—should it be me?* But what of the risks? Images of my husband, Ed, and my two children, Douglas, twelve, and Julie, nine, flashed through my mind. Didn't I have a greater responsibility to them?

But the man needed help. I was fairly trembling with the force of my inner uncertainty. I don't know how long I continued to stand there with the others, my hands gripping the railing as though to keep me from bursting apart. Then, suddenly, I was running down the stairs that led to the dock. *Surely*, I thought, *someone else will have gone in to help. I'll just stand by to pull them out.*

Though I was running, stripping off my sweater and kicking off my shoes as I cleared the dock, it wasn't until I was actually lowering myself into the water, slowly and gingerly, that I realized I was the only help the dockman would be getting.

The water had a brackish taste and an unhealthy odor. I was afraid of the cold and I recoiled from all the filth floating on the surface. The icy water seemed to squeeze me like a fist, forcing out the air from my lungs.

The most sensible thing seemed to be to go for the life ring. Immediately, as I started to swim, the risk of what I was doing overwhelmed me—what if I were never to see my husband or children again? I had heard of drowning men panicking, pulling down their would-be rescuers with them. Or what if my muscles cramped in the cold water?

But then, instantly, the comforting words of prayers I had known since childhood came to my lips: "Lord God, Lamb of God, Son of the Father, have mercy upon us," I prayed aloud. Every word gave me new courage.

"Good! Good girl!" the dockman in the water shouted to me. "The rope!" he said. "We need the rope!" I looked back to see that his assistant on the dock had finally unraveled the rope and thrown it into the water. But not far enough. I swam over to it, grabbed it and, towing the rope behind me, headed toward the two men.

The weight of my sodden clothes was making every move an effort. I could only imagine the terrible struggle of the dockman as he carried not only his own weight, but that of a semi-conscious man.

"Lord have mercy, Christ have mercy, Lord have mercy,"

I repeated with every stroke, praying I would reach the two men before the dockman's strength gave out.

"Put it under his arms," he said to me as I approached. "Loop it under and swim back with your end."

Treading water, my hands shaking with cold, I somehow managed to carry out his instructions.

"Is it all right?" I asked him through chattering teeth. "Are you going to be okay?"

"Yeah. Just get back there as fast as you can!"

I headed back, praying constantly. Ahead of me I could see that a fire-rescue squad and an ambulance had finally arrived. *Thank God.* Now I knew that we'd all be pulled out.

Reaching the dock, I handed my end of the rope to a waiting fireman and then clung to one of the dock's support posts, exhausted. Another fireman reached down, grabbed me by the beltloops of my jeans and pulled me onto the dock. Wrapping a blanket around my shivering shoulders and patting me on the back, he said, "Thanks for doing my job."

I didn't understand what he meant at first. "What?" I said, "Whose job?"

But he just asked, "Are you all right?" I nodded that I was, and, too spent to move, watched as the rescue squad pulled in the drowning man while the dockman held him afloat. In seconds, he was hoisted onto the dock and attended to by the ambulance crews.

When the dockman was pulled out, he just smiled wearily at me. I knew exactly how he felt: too tired for words and a little embarrassed at all the thanks and pats on the back we were getting from the crowd of reporters and photographers who had gathered on the dock.

"Why did you go in?" one of them asked me.

"No one else did."

"But what made you do it?" another asked, apparently unsatisfied with my answer.

"God gave me the strength," I said, a little surprised at my own words.

They wanted to ask more questions, but the firemen were hurrying us into the ambulance. "How do you feel about being a heroine?" I heard as the door closed. *But it wasn't me,* I thought to myself.

On the way to the hospital the dockman and I introduced ourselves—his name was Bob Bergstrom—but we didn't do much talking—our teeth were still chattering. I had time to think about the reporter's questions. Me—a heroine? Although every muscle ached with the effort I had just made, and my whole body trembled with cold under my wet clothes, I felt that I had really done nothing. I was not a brave, strong person, but an ordinary woman with the usual fears and hesitations. I was able to overcome my weakness and jump into the water to help, only because of God's guidance and protection. The mysterious forewarning on the bridge that had been my preparation, the sudden decision to act and the strengthening prayers that attended me in the river—all had come from God.

It was just as St. Paul had written: "I can do all things through Christ which strengtheneth me" (Philippians 4:13).

This was what I wanted to say to the reporters. Never had these words, which I loved so much, taken on such literal meaning. I felt a new peace and humility.

"He's going to survive," one of the attendants said to us as he treated the rescued man. "He's got a broken arm and leg and he's suffering from exposure. But he's going to be all right."

I could see that the man was now conscious, but so chilled he could hardly speak. I silently thanked God for saving his life. Later I learned that he was only twenty-eight years old.

I wrote him a letter, saying that God has a purpose for him in life, but received no answer. Yet I often remember his face, so sad and despondent, and pray that someday he will meet Jesus and feel the saving power of God that can transform weakness and fear into strength.

An Unusual Year for Poinsettias

— Christian Dornbierer —

In May of 1971, our first shipment of poinsettia starter shoots was delivered to our greenhouse. As I helped unload the flats, I wondered if I had ordered more than my customers would need.

I finally managed to submerge that concern with faith in God's guidance. He had led Margaret and me into this work when we had nothing. After several years' struggle we finally had developed our own wholesale flower business. Margaret, our two children and I all loved working with plants. And the flowers used to celebrate the Christian holidays, especially the poinsettias, gave us the most joy.

Poinsettias are sensitive tropical plants that need love in nurturing. The problem lies in growing the right amount, for they are in demand only a few weeks each year. Grow too few and you have disappointed florists who can't satisfy their customers. Too many and you find that poinsettias, as beautiful as they are, do not make good eating. So we depend on intuition.

We began nurturing the fragile four-inch-high sprigs by repotting them in sterilized soil. Then, keeping them at 70 degrees and misting them regularly, we watched them grow into bushy mother plants. In about a month we took cuttings from each plant.

If we were fortunate, they'd take root and become mother plants themselves. As we repeated the process, the poinsettias began to move across the greenhouse racks like a vast green carpet.

Summer cooled into fall and now, as November clouds scurried above, we knew we must make our final decision. Did we have enough plants to satisfy our customers? An inner guidance told me we needed more. From a local grower I ordered a load of a thousand plants. They looked so nice I ordered a thousand more. A few days later he phoned and offered me a third load at an attractive price. On impulse I told him to send them on.

We moved plants to make room. Then I began to worry. One load would be enough. Two was stretching our luck. But three?

I fought those fears by keeping busy. Now we had to be very watchful. The poinsettias would soon bloom as the top leaves, called bracts, slowly turned red. It's vital that they reach full bloom at Christmas. So we control their development by lowering the temperature to hold them back, or raising it to develop them faster.

Then it happened. Out in the greenhouse one morning, a winter's sun warmed my neck as I bent in the rich heady fragrance.

"Chris!" It was Margaret; she had a strange expression on her face. "The phone."

I walked to the phone. On the line was a large Southern grower.

"Your shipment of poinsettias should reach you in a few hours," he said. "Will someone be there?"

I stared dumbly into the phone. Suddenly it all rushed back. Last spring I had decided to try this man's stock and placed a sizable order over the phone. I had completely forgotten it!

Sweat beaded on my forehead. "No! No!" I wanted to shout. "I already have too many!" A battle raged within me. I had a legal right to refuse them. I hadn't signed anything. But I had given my word.

The huge trailer truck strained into our little driveway. By more squeezing and reorganizing, we finally found room. I signed the slip, the truck thundered off, and Margaret and I stood looking at all the poinsettias.

What had I done? I remembered something from the Bible about a man must "keep a promise even if it ruins him" (Psalm 15:4, TLB). My forgetfulness now threatened to wash out all our work. Panic welled within me.

A leaf brushed my hand. I looked down at it. A blush of crimson was on the leaf. And I thought of the legend of this flower—how a poor Mexican boy on his way to the shrine of the Nativity had no gift to offer the Christ Child, nothing but a graceful weed he had found in the forest. But as he placed his gift before the altar with all his love, the top leaves miraculously turned flame red, making it a dazzling flower.

These were His flowers, each one a reminder of His presence.

"Margaret," I said, "we'd better raise the temperature for this batch if they're going to bloom in time."

Two weeks passed and then it was time for florists to phone in their orders. They came in the usual trickle at first. Joe, who always seemed to call early, asked for his usual hundred.

Then, as Christmas shopping picked up, more orders came in. Joe phoned for another load. Now repeat orders began to flow in from everywhere.

It turned out to be an unusual year for poinsettias.

By Christmas Eve our greenhouse was bare. Aching with fatigue, I walked into our living room and slumped into a chair by the Christmas tree to dream into its lights—and to thank God again for His Son who taught us to have faith and to remember that "a man's heart deviseth his way: but the Lord directeth his steps" (Proverbs 16:9).

Dream Warning
— Edward Cushing —

When I arrive at the scene, the old frame house on Chicago's South Side is burning furiously. Smoke and embers dance crazily in the windy winter night. I give the order to unroll the hoses and then dash madly inside. I pull out three people and administer CPR to two of them before the ambulance arrives, rubber screeching on asphalt. When the blaze is finally under control someone from the Department comes up to me. "You did a great job, Captain Cushing," he says, "but two of those three people you pulled out didn't make it."

"No!" I cry. "They're all alive!"

"I'm sorry, Cushing."

Suddenly I awoke in a drenching sweat, my heart racing. My wife, Rosemary, was awake too, staring at me. "Honey, what's wrong?" she asked. "You were shouting."

"Nothing," I mumbled, focusing my eyes. The clock read 4:30 A.M. "Just a bad dream." I fell back on my pillow. I had to get some rest. The following day was Christmas Eve, and I was scheduled for duty.

I was assigned to a single firehouse that quartered Engine 91, a hose company. In Chicago, firemen work three successive twenty-four-hour shifts, living at the firehouse during that time. I'd have under my command three fire fighters and an engineer to monitor the equipment. I was a little nervous. Because of all the holiday leaves, my company had some unseasoned men. I hoped nothing major developed.

By the time I arrived at work the next morning I'd completely forgotten about the dream. In fact, I was happy to find out that my relief engineer had just been promoted, so he must not have been quite as unseasoned as I had feared. Still I was apprehensive. The holidays are a busy time for fire fighters. People get careless during all the excitement. *God*, I prayed, *watch over our city on this wonderful night.*

The shift passed uneventfully. Then, one minute before Christmas, an alarm came in. We manned the engine and roared out of the garage, our siren piercing the night. The blaze was only a half mile from the firehouse, on North Drake Avenue. We were a block away when I spotted smoke. Fire was raging through an old frame house. I called in a second alarm for more equipment and a chief.

We pulled to a stop and I ordered the engineer to hook up both lines and send water through immediately. The first priority was to get the water moving. Then I directed my two other fire fighters to grab lines from the hose beds. "Move!" I shouted.

I approached the house. The policeman who had called in the alarm was hammering on the locked front door. "There are people inside," he panted. Through a dingy pane of glass I could dimly see the outline of a body lying in the hallway. "Step back," I told the cop.

I battered my way in. I lifted the body into my arms. It was a woman. She'd probably been overcome by smoke while trying to escape. I wondered if there were kids. Peering through the smoky darkness I could see that the whole downstairs was afire. I was on my way out with the woman when I spotted the second body. It looked like a child's.

Outside I ordered a fire fighter to get the child. I directed another to go in with a line and start fighting the blaze. I put the woman down in a snow bank. Her eyes were fixed and dilated and I could get no carotid pulse. I'd be back to work on her, but first I went to help with the child, a boy of about seven or eight. We put him down next to the woman. He still had a heartbeat.

I started CPR on the woman. It was a cold, icy night, but perspiration streaked from under my helmet. It had taken us only a minute to reach the scene. A person isn't clinically dead until at least six minutes have passed without oxygen, so I figured we had a fair shot at saving this woman.

I tilted her head back, cleared the breathing passage and gave her five quick breaths followed by fifteen chest compressions. I repeated the steps. No response.

In the background the wail of sirens rose from the night. The fire fighter inside called out that the main fire was centered in the front room. I ordered him all the way in to fight it. An instant later I saw one of the hoses a few feet away, bulging from water pressure, snaking rapidly toward the house.

The chief's buggy arrived. The woman still wasn't responding and my efforts were getting frantic. I rubbed snow on her face. "Come on, lady. You can do it."

"What do you have?" the chief snapped as he knelt by my side.

"I've got two people out and one fire fighter inside on a line by himself. I need a couple of ambulances."

The chief nodded. Then he peered at the woman. "You'd better give up on her," he said. "She's gone."

"No," I said, pounding her chest. "She still has a chance!" Then, exhausted and frightened, I silently called out. *God, bring her back! I've done all I know how. Only You can help now.* A split second later I felt her heart pound against my hand. *Thank You, God.*

Sinking back on my heels, I stared up at the blazing structure. Three people. There were three people in my dream.

Someone else is in there!

I dashed back into the house. My men would have found any additional victims on the ground floor, so I headed through the smoke toward the stairs. I climbed them slowly, sweeping my flashlight ahead of me. Near the top, I spotted him—a boy lying on his back, unconscious.

He had no carotid pulse. His eyes were dilated. I scooped him up and blew into his mouth, giving him fast cardiac compressions with the fingers of my left hand. I carried him down the steps and outside. As I knelt to lay the boy next to his mother, I felt his heart turn over like a tiny motor. He was alive.

After the fire was out and we were putting away our equipment, the chief returned to the scene from the hospital. He took me aside.

"You did a great job, Captain. But I'm afraid the woman and the little boy aren't going to make it."

"Chief," I said "no one is going to die." I didn't explain about the dream. He wouldn't have believed me.

Christmas morning I called the hospital. All three were stable but suffering from smoke inhalation. I was put through to the woman. I told her I'd been at the scene and asked her what she remembered.

"Well," she said, her voice raspy from the smoke, "I was asleep on the couch when one of the boys started screaming that our Christmas tree was on fire. I tried to get everybody out. The last thing I remember is everything going red. Then it turned to a beautiful white. I heard chanting, like music in church. I was very, very peaceful. Suddenly I saw an older man looking into my face. That's when I woke up outside. They told me one of the older firemen rescued me."

"Ma'am, that was me," I said.

She began thanking me but I cut her short. I told her about the dream. "That dream was a warning, a message not to give up on you and to go back in and find the boy. I didn't save you. God did."

That's all I wanted to say. I wasn't the hero. I'd been told what to do on Christmas Eve when I was awakened by the most vivid dream of my life. In a sense, like all good fire fighters, I was just following orders.

GOD'S POWER PROVIDES FOR US

The young lions suffer want and hunger,
but those who seek the Lord lack no good thing.
—Psalm 34:10 (NRSV)

God is able to provide you with every blessing in
abundance. . . .
—II Corinthians 9:8 (NRSV)

A Load of Coal

— H. N. Cook as told to his daughter Patsy C. Godsey —

On Christmas Eve 1948, the snow was coming down hard, blowing and swirling around my old two-ton dump truck as I drove across the West Virginia mountains. It had been snowing for hours and had accumulated eight to ten inches deep. My job at that time was delivering coal to the miners who lived in the coal camp. I had finished early and was looking forward to getting home.

As I neared the road that led to my home, I was flagged down by my stepfather. He told me about a mother with three children who lived about six miles up in the mountains. Her husband had died several months previously, leaving her and the children destitute. In the tradition of taking care of our own, the miners had assembled several boxes of food, clothing and gifts that they wanted me to deliver, along with a load of coal, to the family.

Now believe me, I didn't want to go. Let's face it, I had worked hard all day, it was Christmas Eve, and I wanted to get home to my family. But that was just it—it was Christmas

Eve, the time of giving and goodwill. With this thought in mind, I turned the truck around and drove back to the coal tipple, where I filled the truck. When I returned, I loaded boxes in the front seat and in every nook and cranny I could find in the back. Then I set off.

Back in the hills of West Virginia, folks had built homes in some pretty out-of-the-way places. This woman's place was really out of the way. I had to travel on a road that had not been cleared by the highway department, nor had any path been made by traffic. I drove up the valley as I had been directed, and turned off the road into a hollow called Lick Fork. The "road" was actually a snow-filled creek bed. When I saw that, I began to have doubts that I could make it. Nevertheless, I shifted into first gear and crept ahead.

When I came to the place a mile farther on where I was supposed to turn into the mountain to get to the woman's house, my heart dropped. There before me was a winding path that had been hand-cut up the side of the mountain. I still could not see her house. I pulled the truck up to the path and got out. After looking the situation over, I decided there was no way I could get that two-ton dump truck up through that path.

What am I to do? I wondered. *Maybe I can just dump the coal and ask the family to come down for the food and clothes.* So I got out and walked up the path. It was near dusk, the temperature had dropped, and the blowing snow was beginning to drift.

The path was about six feet wide, overhung with snow-covered branches and littered with stumps and limbs. Finally I reached the clearing where the house stood, a little shack with thin walls and cracks you could see through. I called the woman out of the house, explained why I was there, and asked if she had any way to carry the food and coal. She showed me a homemade wagon with wheelbarrow wheels.

Here I was in ten inches of snow, with a truck I had to empty before dark, an impassable path and a wagon with wheelbarrow wheels. The only solution, as I could see it, was to turn the truck around, back it in as far as I could, dump the coal and set the boxes off.

As I returned to the truck, I kept asking, "Lord, what am I doing here?"

I started up the engine, turned my old truck around and went into reverse. Foot by foot that old truck backed up along that mountain path. I kept telling myself, "I'll just keep going until I can't go any farther."

However, the truck seemed to have a mind of its own. All at once, I was sitting there in the dark with my taillights reflecting through the snow on that little shack. I was dumbfounded. That old truck had not slipped one inch or got stuck one time. And standing on the porch were four of the happiest people I had ever seen.

I unloaded the boxes and then dumped the coal, shoveling as much as I could under the sagging porch. As I worked, the thin, ill-clothed children dragged and pushed the boxes into the shack. When I had finished, the woman grasped my hand and thanked me over and over.

After the good-byes, I got into the truck and started back. Darkness had overtaken me. However, upon reaching the "road," I stopped the truck and looked back at the path. "There is no way," I said to myself, "that I could have maneuvered this truck up that mountain, through all that snow, in the dark, without help from somewhere."

I had been raised to worship God. I believed in the birth of Christ. And that Christmas Eve, in the hills of West Virginia, I knew I had been an instrument of what Christmas is all about.

He Passed the Test
— Patricia Walworth Wood —

Ten-year-old Billy Foy was busy with his homework in the family's mobile home outside of Albany, Indiana. His mother was at work and his father was out in the barn working on a tractor. Suddenly Duke, the mutt at Billy's side, began barking and jumping at the window.

"Calm down, Duke," Billy said. He looked to see if someone was outside or if a cat or a squirrel was racing up a tree. Nothing. But Duke went on running from the window to the door. "Okay, okay," Billy said as he got up and let the dog out. There was something about the way Duke raced straight to the barn, barking all the way, that made Billy follow him.

In the barn Billy was shocked at what he found. A seven hundred-pound steel bracket had fallen off the tractor and pinned his father to the floor.

Billy started to run back to the phone to call for help. "No," his father gasped, fighting for words, "get a jack."

Billy had worked with his father and knew how to operate

the equipment. He used a hydraulic jack to raise the heavy bracket. Then with a floor jack he lifted the bracket enough for his father to roll out. "Thank God you came," Mr. Foy said to his son. "I was about to black out."

While recovering in the hospital, Billy Foy's father was told about what Duke had done. Mr. Foy had not wanted another dog and so Duke had been with them "on trial." He'd only been there three days.

He's been there ever since.

The Waterspout

— Joan Shelton —

On vacation in Mexico, my husband, Dick, and I rigged our Windsurfers on the beach and sailed into the Caribbean.

Dick was several hundred yards ahead of me when suddenly the wind picked up and flipped me into the ocean. By the time I swam back to my board, we were in the midst of a tropical storm.

I tried to pull the sail out of the water, but the wind and rain overpowered me. I couldn't find Dick anywhere. I clung to the board, knowing if I lost hold of it I could drown.

Just then, in the swirling rain, I saw an enormous cruise ship headed directly toward me. I would never be able to get out of its way! Paralyzed with fear, I thought of our two young children back home and closed my eyes in prayer, *Lord, save me.*

When I opened my eyes, the ship was veering away.

As the sea calmed Dick sailed toward me. "Let's get to shore while we can," he said.

Nearing the beach I spotted a friend of ours waving his

arms in a frenzy. Before I was out of the water he called out, "Did you see it?"

"What?" I asked.

"The waterspout. It went across the water, right toward you. Then, just like that," he snapped his fingers, "it disappeared."

Is that why the cruise ship turned? I'll never know. I only know that in my time of need, God answered my prayer.

God's Picker-Upper

— Nancy Bayless —

The first day my husband, Lynn, received chemotherapy for bone-marrow cancer, I was overwhelmed with sadness. We live on a boat, and that night I worried about him and all the work that was now my responsibility.

At midnight as I was preparing for bed, I ran out of paper towels. In the darkness of the main cabin I found a new double package in a locker. I ripped open the cellophane and took out a roll. I always buy plain white to go with our red-white-and-blue decor. In the light I could see this roll was covered with pink flowers—all wrong!

Somehow that did it. I burst into tears. "Lord, I can't even buy the right paper towels!" I wallowed in self-pity, wailing to God. How will I varnish the boat? How will I maintain the engine? How will I go on without Lynn?

Finally my tears were spent. I picked up the roll of paper towels, and as I put it in the holder I noticed there was writing among the pink flowers. One sheet read "Friendship is a special gift." Those words made me think of all the friends I could call on at any hour. The next words were "Love is sharing." I thought of the gifts we had been given—casseroles, cookies, hugs. Then "No act of love however small is ever wasted" reminded me of the telephone calls and other kindnesses we had received. I felt at peace.

The next morning I opened the locker again. Inside the torn cellophane was the second roll of paper towels—not covered with flowers. It was plain white.

When the Word Became Real

— Richard Trufitt —

"Daddy, please read us a bedtime story," four-year-old Samantha said.

"Story," echoed her sister, Lisa, two.

I chose a book with lots of pictures and sat down between my daughters. Then, as I'd done so many times before, I set my imagination to work as I turned the pages.

I was thirty-four years old, and ever since my wife left me, I had raised our girls alone. With my steady job as an electrician, I was capable of providing for them, but I worried that I wouldn't be the kind of parent they could look up to. How would they react when they realized that their daddy couldn't read?

It wasn't that I hadn't tried to learn. I loved learning new things, and in school I had listened extra hard to soak up as much knowledge as I could. Mathematics and science were my passions, and I was fascinated by electricity. I set up complicated electrical projects at home. But I rarely passed a written test in school.

My mother tried tutoring me. I could follow a simple sentence, such as "The cat sat on the mat." But I stumbled over anything more challenging, losing the sense of the phrases I struggled to put together. One day I sat at the kitchen table, a book open in front of me. Frustrated, my mother snapped, "You're just like your father. He couldn't read either." I stared at the lines of forbidding black print, ashamed. From then on I stopped trying. Year to year I scraped by, barely advancing to the next grade. Finally I dropped out of school when I was fifteen years old.

Something inside told me I wasn't stupid. And because I had to concentrate hard, listen well and rely on memory, my mind became like a computer. After a five-year apprenticeship with an electrician, I had become extremely skilled at what I did.

But at home I felt inadequate. When Lisa or Samantha caught a cold or got a fever, I couldn't even read the advice in Dr. Spock's child-care book. And how would I be able to help them with their homework?

There was something else I wanted to give them—a good moral background. I could teach them how to rewire a house or explain the most complicated properties of electricity. But I knew nothing about religion and I didn't know where to start.

"That's easy," my baby-sitter said one afternoon when I asked her advice. "It's all in the Bible."

"I've never learned anything from a book," I said. "Me and books don't get along too well."

"Some friends of mine hold a Bible study twice a week," she said. "They don't just read the Bible; they talk about it. Maybe you can join them on Tuesday."

I'd do anything for my girls, so I went. "I'm just here to listen," I announced to the group. One of the members read a passage aloud and then everybody discussed it. Several people described how God worked in their lives just as he worked in the lives of the biblical characters. I was skeptical. I'd never heard people talk like this before.

Still, I was attracted by the loving atmosphere and went back that Thursday. When my turn came to read, I signaled for them to pass the Bible on. They knew I couldn't read.

One Tuesday night when I got home, I tucked the girls into bed and told them about the passage we'd just read, the story of Jonah and the whale. "Did the big fish eat Jonah up, Daddy?" Samantha asked. But our group hadn't gotten to the end yet. "To be continued," I told the girls.

In the last few minutes of our sessions, members asked God's help in all sorts of ways. A woman needed a better car, a man needed a job. Curious, I made a mental note of the problems that each one mentioned. At future meetings, I'd take the petitioners aside and ask if God had answered their prayers. I kept score.

I doubted that prayer held the answer to my problem. I'd wrestled with reading long enough to know that it would never yield to some simple solution. And besides, why would God answer my prayer?

One night during the petitions, a man gave thanks for his

new job. "It's perfect," he said. "Thank you for praying for me." This gave me an idea: I didn't believe *my* prayers would be answered, but maybe God would hear the prayers of my friends. I trusted their strong faith. After all, the scorecard I'd been keeping leaned heavily on the side of answered prayers.

At the next meeting, I sat quietly through the discussion, trying to summon my courage. When it was time for prayer requests, I spoke up. "I want to read," I said. My friends prayed with me. Then I put it out of my mind. I didn't want to be disappointed.

A few weeks later, the woman next to me at the meeting read from the Bible. We had a lively discussion, and I was finally comfortable with taking part. When the Bible was passed, this time, for some inexplicable reason, my hands reached for it. Somehow this book was different from all the others. I wanted to touch it, hold it in my hands. The binding was warm, its leather darkened from handling. I thought about the knowledge that we had shared. I was holding the fount of that knowledge. The pages were creased, edges a bit ragged from anxious fingers searching for answers and hope. My neighbor pointed to the place where she had paused.

"Take your time," someone said softly. I took a deep breath, and as I exhaled, my fear began to melt away. The book seemed to say, *Read me. Drink me in.* I was thirsty for God's Word. I had never wanted anything so strongly in my life. I put my finger on the place where we had left off.

Slowly, haltingly, I began. As my finger followed the lines of print, those collections of letters became words that I understood. I was actually doing what I had not been able to do before. I was reading!

After a few sentences I stopped. The group was absolutely silent. When I looked up, they began to clap. A loud thunderous clap. I heard God in their clapping. He was working in my life. Because when I let God come into my heart, he also opened my mind. His Word had become real.

GOD'S PURPOSES
COORDINATE US

My times are in thy hand. . . .
—Psalm 31:15

God, who comforts the downcast,
comforted us by the coming of Titus.
—II Corinthians 7:6 (RSV)

MY ACADEMIC HOOD

— Paul Heller —

When I graduated from seminary, I acquired a handsome three-foot-long purple-red-gold-and-black academic hood signifying the degree I'd earned. As a Presbyterian minister I wore it over my black robe for special ceremonies, ordinations and installations.

One day I opened my closet and it was not there. I couldn't remember when I'd last worn it or where I'd left it, but I quickly prayed that it was not lost.

At the time, I was pastor of a small congregation in the western hills of New York's huge Adirondack Forest Preserve. Then I was extended a call to serve as minister of a larger congregation in a more urban area on the shores of Lake Champlain. After considerable soul-searching, I accepted the call, but I prayed for reassurance that my decision was the right one.

I was greeted warmly by the staff and congregation at the new church. I had fond memories of a visit I had made there eight years earlier for an installation ceremony, but it was only when I opened the closet door in my new office that I knew

I had done the right thing in coming to this church, this time to stay.

There I discovered my hood, waiting for me as it had waited patiently for eight years.

Plum Perfect

— Nancy Taylor —

Daddy planted his plum tree with the idea that it would produce luscious purple plums—the tiny, sugary kind, perfect for making wine. But while Daddy hoped for the harvest, Mama and I prayed against it.

Back then, a dozen years ago, Daddy grew almost all his fruits and vegetables for homemade wine. The patio was lined with bottles of tomato wine, sweet-potato wine and cucumber-carrot wine. Now he awaited the season when he could add his new and potent plum wine.

By making his own concoctions, Daddy rationalized, his drinking wasn't harmful. He was wrong. The plum tree grew, and so did the control alcohol had over Daddy's life. What had begun as an occasional glass of beer or a jigger of Polish vodka with Grandpa on holidays was destroying him—and our family.

The plum tree sprouted snowy white blossoms every spring. By summertime, we saw a few young plums, but the birds devoured them. In fact, year after year the tree failed to bear fruit. "Thank You, Lord," Mama would whisper.

Finally Daddy's drinking got so bad that he had to be hospitalized. Afterward, he went to a treatment center. Slowly, almost miraculously, his spiritual strength grew. Today he is becoming a gentle and loving father.

Last spring, the plum tree blossomed as usual. The fruit began to appear, green at first, then turning to garnet. As the plums ripened, the birds helped themselves—but the tree remained full and the branches bowed under the weight of the fruit! It was time for the long-awaited harvest, at last.

Mama and I helped Daddy pick his luscious purple plums—the tiny, sugary kind, perfect for making jam.

"No Hot Chocolate?"

— Cheryl Morrison —

"No hot chocolate on Christmas Eve?" our teenage daughter, Christine, asked. I looked away.

"Next year," I promised as she went to get ready for the midnight service.

We'd always had hot chocolate on Christmas Eve; it was a tradition. But this year we couldn't afford even that simple item. When my husband, Jack, was laid off six months earlier, he started a claims-adjusting business, working out of our basement. But the response had been dreadful, and it didn't help when our car's transmission died. Our older daughter, Janice, contributed her earnings from her first full-time job, and the girls never complained about doing without. Still, as the year drew to a close, our financial picture looked bleaker and bleaker.

As we headed out the door, my eyes fell on our old artificial tree draped with last year's dulled tinsel. *And I couldn't even squeeze money for hot chocolate out of our budget*, I thought. During the service, I prayed silently, *O, Lord, You promised to take care of us. Have You forgotten?*

Everyone except me, it seemed, was uplifted by the message of hope in the service. At its close, people hugged and shook hands. As we bundled up in coats and scarves, Christine's youth counselor called to us: "Wait!" She pulled a ribboned jar from her bag. "Merry Christmas." She had brought us hot chocolate mix!

She hadn't known about our family tradition. And she didn't know that, to me, this simple gift was a reminder that God had not forgotten us after all.

The Sweater

— Becky Alexander —

Late in World War II my father was on the battlefront in Germany. In March 1945, while his Canadian regiment awaited supplies, Dad was ordered to Aldershot, England, to be decorated by King George VI.

The weather was raw in Aldershot, but Dad had given away his regulation greatcoat to a soldier back at the front. Shivering, he headed straight for the Red Cross center and picked from a bin full of sweaters a thick hand-knit one with a double collar. It fit perfectly under his tunic, warming him without breaking the uniform code.

After receiving the Military Medal for bravery, at Buckingham Palace, Dad rejoined the regiment and was issued another coat. He packed the sweater away in his kit.

Dad returned home safely to Canada in January 1946. His mother was glad to do his laundry again. While sorting his clothes, she held up the sweater, amazed. Then to my father's astonishment, she grabbed a pair of scissors and snipped the collar.

Like many women during the war, Grandma had knit sweaters for the young men overseas. She always put a note and postage money inside, so they could write back. "I prayed for the boys who would receive my handiwork, asking God to guide them safely home," she said. Many corresponded with her for years after.

While her hands had faithfully knitted, other Hands had guided her son safely home. Inside the collar of the sweater was some postage money—and a note she had written to a boy overseas.

Just in Time

— Pat Hrabe Wehrli —

My five-year-old son and I were driving the lonely ten-mile stretch from town to our home, when we hit a bump and heard the *thump-thump* of a flat tire.

I began digging out tools from the trunk and discovered we had no tire iron. There I was, a very pregnant young woman standing beside a crippled car with a child in the front seat.

In the past year several local women had been brutally murdered, and the authorities had no idea who the killer was. When a man in a pickup stopped to ask if I needed help, I felt only fear. "That's all right," I said. "My husband is on his way." In fact, my husband, Gerald, wouldn't be coming along this road for at least another hour.

To my relief the man drove off. I looked at the distant houses along the highway, trying to decide what to do.

Minutes later, I saw the stranger coming back our way. He stopped on the other side of the highway and slowly walked toward us. *Dear Lord*, I prayed, *protect my children.* Just as he reached us Gerald pulled up.

"There's my husband now," I said, surprised to see that he had been let off work early. Gerald parked, glancing at the stranger, who left in a hurry.

More than a year later an area resident confessed to the unsolved murders. As a reserve officer for the county sheriff's department, Gerald escorted the prisoner from the county jail to the mental health center.

The instant he saw the suspect, Gerald recognized him. It was the stranger who had stopped by my car.

The Guitar Lesson

— Jeanne Breaugh —

When our son David was twelve we took him to a symphony concert featuring a classical guitarist. After that his one great goal in life was to play classical guitar.

He practiced constantly. He idolized the Spanish master AndrÄs Segovia and dreamed of meeting him. He wanted to own a fine Ramirez guitar—far too expensive for us. He aspired to become a professional musician. I was proud of him, but also worried. His dreams were so big. "Lord," I prayed, "don't let him down."

In 1974, when David was thirteen, I found out that Segovia was coming to Chicago's Orchestra Hall. From Lansing, Michigan, where we live, I sent away for tickets, requesting one seat near the stage for our young aficionado. We received four tickets in the back balcony and one front-row center!

The concert was the thrill of a lifetime. From our balcony seats I could look down through my opera glasses and see David in the front row. His eyes never left the stage. Afterward he rushed backstage to meet the eighty-year-old maestro. A short time later David joined us in the lobby, empty-handed.

"I was next in line, Mom," he said, "when his secretary said Segovia was tired and wouldn't be signing any more programs."

I was crushed. *How could You do this to him, God?* I wondered.

The next day, we toured the Sears Tower and browsed through the shops on Michigan Avenue. All the while I couldn't get over the disappointment of the night before.

Finally, we drove to an outlet where Ramirez guitars were sold, just so David could see one. At the correct address we couldn't find a sign for the store—just a rickety staircase. I waited in the car while David and his father went up.

Minutes later, David came rushing down. "Give me the program from last night!" he said, breathless.

I gave him the program and followed him inside. There was the maestro, shaking David's hand! For several minutes the two talked about David's music, and then the owner of the store asked our son, "Could you walk Mr. Segovia down the stairs?"

As he watched the two of them leave, the owner said to me: "This is the first time Segovia has been to the store in years. Usually we send our instruments to him."

That was the day I learned to trust God with the big dreams of my guitarist son, who later played in a master class with Segovia, and eventually performed at Orchestra Hall—with a Ramirez guitar.

The Right Solo
— Mary Wheatley Van Hoosen —

WANTED: ONE SOPRANO FOR SUMMER POSITION. This notice appeared in the church bulletin on a Sunday morning in 1945. I was new in Washington, D.C., and I wanted to be chosen for that job. I lost no time in presenting myself to the choir director, who set up an audition for me on the following Sunday.

After a lot of thought and prayer I selected Geoffrey O'Hara's "I Walked Today Where Jesus Walked" for my audition piece. All week long I practiced. But back at the church on Sunday I made the dreadful discovery that I'd left the music on the bus. And then, to add to my disappointment, the choir director whom I thought I'd be singing for was not there. He had been called out of town, and the decision about my hiring was now up to someone else. As it turned out, the substitute organist and choir director was a friendly sixtyish gentleman who put me at ease immediately.

Even so I hesitated. Finally I had to tell him that I'd lost my music. "What piece were you planning to sing?" he asked.

" 'I Walked Today Where Jesus Walked,' " I told him. Assuring me he could play it from memory, he launched into the accompaniment.

"You sang that exactly as it should be sung," my accompanist told me after I'd finished. "Welcome to the choir."

I was overjoyed. Only when I was leaving did I think to ask his name. With a mischievous grin, the organist—and noted composer—replied, "Geoffrey O'Hara."

GOD'S MESSAGES
DIRECT US

The Lord is my shepherd. . . .
He leads me in right paths
for his name's sake.
—Psalm 23:1, 3 (NRSV)

During the night Paul had a vision. . . .
—Acts 16:9 (NRSV)

Take the Time

— Barbara Deal —

While finishing up a one-day business trip to Los Angeles, my husband, Bob, and I discovered that our meeting site was about ten minutes from my grandmother's nursing home. We had only an hour before boarding our flight home to Walla Walla, hardly enough time to visit her. But something deep within me said, *Take the time.*

We hadn't seen Grandma in years, not since her mind began to fail. She didn't recognize her own son, or remember that her husband was dead. Surely she wouldn't know us. We planned to be back in L.A. in a few months and could spend more time with her then. *Why go now?* I asked myself as we made our way through L.A. traffic. I looked at my watch.

At the nursing home, we found Grandma asleep in her wheelchair. I walked over and gently touched her on the shoulder. "Grandma? Grandma?"

She awoke, blinked a few times and looked hard at me. Then her eyes filled with wonder. "Barbara? Is that really you?" Grandma not only recognized Bob and me, she was absolutely lucid! She wanted to know everything about us. We reminisced about the times I had stayed with her when I was a child. The trips we made to Yosemite every summer. We talked about my grandfather. About what she thought heaven must be like. And how much she wanted to go there, to be with him again.

I had forgotten all about the time until Bob reminded me we had a plane to catch. Grandma hugged us and saw us off.

The day after we got home, my father called to say that Grandmother had had a massive stroke. The next morning, she slipped into heaven.

It would have been so easy not to stop and see Grandma that day. But we'd obeyed that nudge of the Spirit. And an hour had become a lifelong memory.

All She Asked For

— Shirley Wilcox —

The gladioli in my garden were in full bloom. On my way to visit my mother in the retirement home, I cut three tall stalks and wrapped them in a damp paper towel and waxed paper. Purple and lush, the flowers would make a beautiful bouquet for her room.

When I reached the home I passed through the lobby and walked toward Mother's room in the G wing. Suddenly I stopped and turned around and headed down another hall to the nursing unit.

I had no idea why I had changed direction, and I cannot tell you why at the nurses' station I asked to be directed to Mrs. Farmer's room. I only knew Mrs. Farmer as the elderly lady who sat ramrod straight in front of me at church on Sunday mornings, wearing brightly colored hats on her snowy white hair. I hadn't seen her for several months, and didn't remember hearing that she was ill.

The door to Mrs. Farmer's room was open. She was lying in bed, her face toward the window, her eyes closed. Her thin, bony arms lay outstretched on the white coverlet.

Mrs. Farmer opened her eyes and turned, not in the least surprised. "Oh, thank you for remembering my birthday," she exclaimed. Then gazing at the gladioli bouquet, she added, "That's all I asked for."

I put the flowers in a vase on her bedside table and left quietly. I walked down the hall with a mixed feeling of gratitude and awe.

Those "Nonexistent" Signs

— Marlene Wiechman —

Coming back from a vacation trip, my family and I were driving along a desolate stretch of highway in Wyoming when our daughter, Emily, who was almost five, suddenly said she felt sick.

Right away I knew something was terribly wrong. Her eyes kept shifting, and when I coaxed her, she would briefly bring them back into focus. "Emily!" I called to her. And then she lost consciousness.

"Lord," I prayed, "we need to get her to a doctor fast." The nearest town was Rock Springs, about sixty miles away. Every minute was precious. Emily had had a stroke when she was seven months old and we were always on the alert for any signs of another one.

At last we were nearing Rock Springs. Once there though, how would we find a doctor? To our relief, we spotted a blue sign with a white "H" on it. And soon after that, another sign, then another directing us to the hospital where Emily was ushered into the emergency room. Soon her condition stabilized, and improved rapidly. A mild epileptic seizure, the doctor said.

That afternoon my husband and my father drove out to the highway to a gas station we'd seen—and got lost coming back to the hospital. They had been counting on the hospital signs to guide them. When they told the doctor of their misadventure, he said, "What signs? There are no hospital signs on that road."

And yet we had seen those signs—just when they were needed most.

"Please Hurry—I'm Hurt!"

— Rose Lear —

My son did not come home that foggy night. Justin, almost eighteen, had gone out in his car with a friend on Friday evening, August 6, 1993. At first I hadn't worried. He was a good boy, a careful driver and always dependable. He knew he had to be up early Saturday morning for his summer job cleaning pools.

I went to bed thinking I'd hear Justin arrive home any minute. As always, I prayed for him, his twenty-year-old brother, Strider, and my older sister, Mary Beth, who lives with us.

I awoke Saturday morning with a start. Justin! I hadn't heard him come in. Heart pounding, I jumped out of bed and checked his room. Then I rushed into the kitchen, where Mary Beth was making coffee.

"Justin didn't come home!" I announced.

The percolator trembled in Mary Beth's hand. She loves her nephews dearly. "Where do you suppose he is?"

"I don't know. He always calls, even if he's delayed a short time."

"Maybe he stayed over at his friend's house," Mary Beth suggested.

I hurried to the phone on the desk in the kitchen. No, said his friend, Justin had dropped him off last night and headed home to White Bluff from Nashville. That was only about a twenty-minute drive.

I started calling everyone he knew, including his high-school football teammates. Fall practice was starting Monday and that was all Justin had talked about recently. As I dialed number after number, I kept glancing out the window, expecting his car to come up the drive. I longed to see his golden retriever, Hunter, bound up to him; to hear Justin explain: "Hi, Mom. I'm sorry; I forgot to call you . . ."

I slumped back after speaking with the last of his friends. No one knew anything. The thoughts I'd been pushing away finally broke through. *He's lying dead somewhere. Someone's hijacked his car. He's been kidnapped.*

I dialed our pastor, Mack Hannah of Harpeth Heights Baptist Church, who said he'd get a prayer chain going immediately. Then I dialed the Dickson County Sheriff's Department. Two deputies came right out.

"He's a little more than six feet tall, brown hair, brown eyes, two hundred twenty-five pounds," I told them. "A big guy, plays football." How could I describe his smile that lighted up a room? His wonderful sense of humor?

"Car? A blue 1980 MGB convertible." They wouldn't be interested in knowing that the car was both a birthday and early graduation present, or how proud he was of it.

As the older deputy wrote down the information, he commented on the unusually heavy fog the night before. Then, as they turned to leave, he patted my shoulder. "We'll do our best to find him, ma'am."

Mary Beth brought me a cup of coffee. "Now don't give up, Rose," she urged. "We're going to find him."

I smiled wryly. That was Mary Beth. Always trying to be optimistic.

But not Strider. He was beside himself with worry. "I can't just sit here, Mom," he said. Instead of going to work, he drove off to look for his brother. Mary Beth went with him.

I sat at the desk staring at the phone. It rang—over and over. But it was our pastor reporting that the entire congregation was praying. Then concerned friends called, asking what they could do to help. I laid my head on my arms. I was divorced from Justin's father; my boys meant everything to me. "God," I prayed, "please don't take my baby. If you need someone, take me."

I felt a touch on my shoulder. It was Mary Beth; she was back from the search.

At my pleading look she shook her head, but tried to cheer me. "Rose," she said, "I just *know* Justin will be all right." She picked up A.J., our cat, who had been pacing around my chair, and cradled her in her arms. "God has his eye on Justin," she said. I gratefully squeezed her hand, but wished I could be as certain.

All the rest of the day the phone kept ringing. The sheriff's office reported that authorities in two counties were combing the area, checking every route Justin might have taken, and that the Tennessee Bureau of Investigation had been notified. Strider went out again to search. It seemed Justin had vanished from the earth.

Mary Beth and I sat up long past midnight praying and dozing fitfully. About 5:30 A.M. I woke up and opened my eyes to find her sitting bolt upright in a chair. "Rose," she said, "a verse—Matthew 7:7—has come to me. 'Ask, and it will be given you; seek, and you will find; knock, and it will be opened to you' [RSV]. That means we can't give up; we have to keep praying."

Finally, in utter exhaustion, we both went to bed to try to get some sleep. I awoke to sunlight flooding the room and went downstairs to resume my vigil. I sat looking at family pictures. There was Justin as a toddler holding a football. Next to that was a photo of Justin as a first grader who stroked my face and told me, "I have the prettiest mommy." I couldn't hold back the tears.

I heard a step on the stairs and looked up. Mary Beth stood there, a strange expression on her face.

"Rose, I know you're going to think I'm crazy," she said, "but I know—I know where Justin is."

I stared at her. What on earth was she talking about?

She sat down across from me. "Justin came to me in a dream," she said. "I could hear him calling to me. It was so plain and clear. He told me where he was. He said, 'I can't move and I need help. Come and get me. I'm between Highway 100 and the railroad tracks. Please hurry—I'm hurt." Her voice was quivering. "I told him we'd be right there."

Strider, who overheard us, rushed into the room. "I know just where that spot is! On Old Harding Road."

I looked at the two of them numbly. Both were clearly exhausted and willing to grasp at anything. "If it will make you feel better, Mary Beth," I said wearily, "you and Strider go look. I'll stay here by the phone."

After they left, the minutes ticked by. I could only stare at my son's picture in his football uniform, wondering if I'd ever see his number sixty-one on the field again.

The phone rang. I barely had the strength to pick up the receiver.

"Rose . . ."

It was Mary Beth, almost shouting with excitement.

"Rose, *we found him!*"

I listened in stunned disbelief as Mary Beth continued breathlessly: "Justin was exactly where he told me he was in my dream—between Highway 100 and the railroad tracks! In the fog, his car went off the curve there and down that steep embankment into a ravine. It was impossible to see him from the highway. He was unconscious and paramedics took him to Baptist Hospital in Nashville."

I hurried to Justin's bedside. He had been wearing his seat belt, but the impact of the accident had thrown him out of the car. He was in a coma, badly scorched from lying unconscious in the sun all Saturday. The doctors said he would have lived only hours if he hadn't been found. Even so, they gave little hope for his recovery.

For five days I sat by Justin's bedside, praying as he

remained in a coma. His friends and teammates came in to cheer him on, hold his hand, and pray for him.

And then on the sixth day he finally opened his eyes. I leaned close to hear his first precious words; and when they came I had to smile. "I'm . . . hungry," he said.

"What can I get you?"

"Two . . . big . . . fat chili dogs." I almost laughed out loud. I knew then that my son would recover.

After months of therapy, Justin was back in high school in January 1994. He remembers nothing about that terrible night, only that the fog had suddenly became so thick he couldn't see.

But all of us who prayed for Justin believe that God allowed that dream to come to Mary Beth, who so implicitly believed in the promise "Ask, and it will be given you."

And seek, and you will find.

Something I Had to Do

— Clara Wallace Nail —

I awoke that morning feeling there was something I had to do. As I went over the day's schedule, my mind fastened on Lena.

Lena lived alone at the end of our road in McDonough, Georgia. Elderly and ill, she depended on friends to help her out. The day before, I had taken her food, but she insisted I didn't need to come back the next day. "I have everything I need right here," she said.

She was proud and dignified and I respected her privacy, but all morning long an inner prompting urged me to go see her. I got the children off to school, loaded the washer, put the breakfast dishes in the sink, but the nagging wouldn't stop. Finally I headed down the road.

On her porch I called her name. Usually she came to the door, but this time there was no answer. Hearing a sound inside, I tried the doorknob and let myself into a living room filled with smoke.

Lena lay on the sofa, too weak to get up. In front of her

was a small coal heater whose door had come off its hinges. Live coals had fallen on the floor and Lena had tried to smother them with quilts, clothes, anything she could reach from the sofa. At any moment they might have burst into flame. I had arrived just in time.

Later, the coals removed and the house cleared of smoke, Lena seemed unusually calm about her near tragedy. "Weren't you afraid?" I asked her.

"No," she said, "I knew you'd come. I prayed."

Turn on the Lights!

— Lucille Lind Arnell —

As a teacher here in Chicago, in a big-city school, I am aware of the concern these days about crime and violence, especially in our larger urban areas. Every night on television I see reports of robberies and shootings. But I am not afraid, because of something that happened to me a number of years ago.

One fall when my husband, Len, was in his third year of seminary, he was serving an internship as preacher in a small midwestern town. Our parsonage was a sun-bleached house next to the white frame church with its tall steeple and wooden sign announcing services. Even though we were city folks, we fit right in, and our parsonage door swung open and shut often.

One evening a woman I'll call Mrs. Mack came to discuss a personal problem. She was a gym teacher in the local high school where I taught math. Her husband was the principal of the elementary school. She wasn't a church member but I hoped our tiny congregation might get a new addition or two.

As I washed dishes I heard Mrs. Mack sobbing and stepped to the living room door to see if I might be needed. Len waved me in.

"He really loves me," cried Mrs. Mack. "It's just that he has this horrible compulsion. The other night, after being away for the weekend, he drove up, brakes screeching, and stomped into the house. He proceeded to terrorize our son and daughter, breaking their toys and yelling, 'You probably love these more than me!'"

I asked if her husband drank. "Oh, no," she said. "He usually acts like this after he comes home from a town about a hundred and fifty miles from here. There is a woman who calls our house every so often, and I see calls to that town on our phone bill. I think he has a problem with her."

She dabbed her eyes with a tissue. Then, looking up, she pleaded, "Reverend, would you drive up there with me? I'm afraid he's in trouble. I have her address."

I could tell this was more than Len had bargained for. "Well," he demurred, "I'll think about it and let you know tomorrow."

We discussed it that evening. Finally Len said, "I feel I should try to help them. Let me see if Larry will come with us." Larry was the minister of a Methodist church in a town north of us. The next day when I arrived home from school, I found a note: "Honey, decided to go. Larry is with us. Don't worry. Should be home after midnight."

A chill went through me. *Trust in God,* I told myself. After all, God was with them.

I managed to get through the evening, first teaching my two piano students, then taking our dog, Charlie, for a walk, and working on some church papers. At ten o'clock I turned out the lights and started for bed.

At that moment I was startled by gravel hitting the house like shotgun pellets as a car roared into our driveway. I put on my robe, went downstairs and tiptoed in the darkness toward the front window.

Suddenly fists pounded on the door and a man's voice roared: "I know you're in there, Mrs. Arnell. I'm Mr. Mack and I've got a gun!"

I froze. In the dim light I could see a man on the porch, his face contorted with rage, holding a gun.

"You listen to me," he barked. "See that car in your driveway? That's my wife's car. I know she drove away with your husband this afternoon, and when they get back I'm going to kill him. Your husband is a womanizer!"

My blood ran cold. "But, Mr. Mack . . ."

He ran down the front steps and crouched behind the evergreens. "I'm going to wait here," he yelled, "and when they pull up, *zingo!*"

I shrank back. What should I do? I started toward the phone to call the police when the front door seemed to explode with pounding.

"Don't you call the police," he raved, "because I'll shoot anyone who comes near—and I'll kill you too before they get me!"

Our phone rang. I grabbed it on the first ring.

It was my husband. "Are you all right, honey?"

"Listen," I whispered, "Mr. Mack is waiting in the shrubbery right outside our front door. He has a gun—" My voice broke. "I think he plans on killing all of us."

Len tried to calm me. "We'll be careful. We found out he has a woman here who claims they're going to get married. We'll be home in about three hours. Meanwhile, I think Mr. Mack is bluffing, but keep the door locked and stay quiet. I love you."

I hung up the phone with a trembling hand. It was nearing midnight.

Pounding thundered on the front door again. "Don't you try anything; I'm still here."

I sank down in a rocker and prayed. "O Lord Jesus, please help me. Please help that poor demented soul out there." In the darkness I cried. I knelt. Then, exhausted, I slumped back into the rocker again.

Suddenly a thought came: *Turn on the lights! Every light in the house. Then go down, unlock the door, explain to Mr. Mack that Len had called and that he is with Mrs. Mack along with another minister, so he doesn't have to worry anymore. And,* the thought commanded, *invite him in.*

"O God, no!" I cried. "I can't do that. He's got a gun. If I admit Len is with his wife he might kill me."

Do it.

With hands shaking, I snapped on every light in the house. Then I opened the front door and said, "Mr. Mack? Mr. Mack?"

The bushes rustled. "Why are all the lights on? Have you called the police?"

"No, Mr. Mack. Pastor Arnell just called. And you are right. Mrs. Mack is with him, along with another minister. They're on their way home right now." I pressed on, trying to keep my voice from quavering. "Put your gun away. You won't need it now. Come inside where it's more comfortable. I'll make some coffee."

Mr. Mack slowly rose from the bushes and came up the front steps. He slid the gun inside his coat as he walked through the front door. Hands pressing his temples, he moaned, "Oh, my head, my head. It hurts so."

"Let me get you some aspirin."

The phone rang. It was a neighbor asking if anything was wrong. Mr. Mack had followed me to the phone; he locked one arm around my neck and, breathing heavily, tried to listen to the party at the other end.

"Oh, the lights," I said. "Yes, Mrs. Johnson, I know it's strange at this hour but we have guests. They'll be leaving soon."

He released me and slumped down on the living room couch, holding his head. I brought him the aspirin, and started making coffee. As it perked I sat with him and talked about his family and our wonderful Lord Jesus, who would help him through his troubles. He seemed to calm a bit. I got the coffee and served it, knowing I had to hold his attention for at least two more hours.

As the mantel clock ticked, I prayed aloud for Mr. Mack,

his family and all of us. I got our Bible and read to him. The more I talked to him the more assurance I seemed to feel. It was as if God was right in the room with us, giving me a sense of peace.

Mr. Mack nodded a bit and I encouraged him to rest.

"No! No!" he shouted, jerking himself upright and feeling under his coat for the gun. I continued talking to him, soothing him, reading from the Bible. Another hour went by, then two. I fought sleep, hoarse from talking and praying. Something seemed to be happening to him, for the rage had subsided. At 4:30 A.M. a car pulled up in the driveway. Mr. Mack jumped to his feet as his wife rushed in through the front door. I was amazed to see her throw her arms around him; the two stood there hugging and crying. I collapsed in a chair, thanking Jesus for being with us.

Mrs. Mack knew her husband needed psychiatric help and persuaded him to enter a hospital. After extensive medical treatment and spiritual counseling, he eventually recovered and returned to his family.

To this day I am awed at the way the Holy Spirit directed me that night, giving me the courage to turn on the lights and invite a distraught, armed man into my home. It was a lesson I will never forget. So today when I see those television reports of crime and violence, I am thankful that I do not have to be afraid. Instead I rely on God for his sure protection.

She Called My Name

— Jake Erdmann —

My wife, Elizabeth, and I were driving home to Racine on a cool, starless night when the motor of our ancient Chevy died and we glided to a halt on a two-lane highway. I got out of the car and saw that there was a slight downward incline ahead of us. "Good," I said, "we can try to jump start the engine."

I asked Elizabeth to get behind the steering wheel. "Press the clutch to the floor," I said. "I'll push with my shoulder against the door. As soon as the car picks up speed, let your foot off the clutch."

Elizabeth wrapped her fingers firmly around the steering wheel. After I got the car rolling, I stepped to the rear to push it from behind. Just then I heard Elizabeth call my name: "Jake!"

I moved quickly to the side of the car and *bam!* A car, speeding so fast that I didn't hear it approach, smashed into the Chevy's rear, hurling me off the road and into unconsciousness.

I woke up in the hospital with a broken shoulder, and other breaks and bruises. Fortunately the three young men in the other car survived, but it took months before my injuries (and Elizabeth's badly sprained ankles) healed. During one bedside visit, Elizabeth told me that both cars had been totaled.

"If I hadn't moved when you called out my name, I would have been totaled too," I said. "What good timing."

Elizabeth was puzzled. "I didn't say anything," she said. "I was so frightened, my lips were clamped shut."

In the Right Direction
— Thelma Leavy —

I have always loved the snow. I'm eighty-five and legally blind, but I can see light and some shapes—and I still get excited by fluffy flakes. That's why I ventured out of my house in Marion, Michigan, late one snowy afternoon last winter.

I shuffled down my long driveway to my favorite Douglas fir. I went from tree to tree, shaking snow from the boughs. Soon I noticed that I was surrounded by vague unfamiliar shapes. I'd gone too far into the woods! I turned and started walking back toward my driveway. But which way had I come? Everything was so white. And cold. The snow fell harder. Wiping tears from my eyes, I rushed forward in a panic. "God," I cried, "please help me."

Abruptly I stopped in my tracks.

I stood perfectly still as a feeling of relief broke through my fear. Then I turned completely around and struck out in a new direction. Finally I came to a fence. It was my boundary line! I followed that fence, just hung to it, until I reached my gate. "Thank You, God," I said.

The next morning, Dan, the young man who shovels snow for me, came rushing in, alarmed by the footsteps he had seen on the snow-covered property. "Don't worry," I quickly explained, "they're mine."

"Mrs. Leavy," Dan said, "I followed those footsteps. They lead up to the edge of the riverbank, right to where the drop-off is steepest. If you'd taken even one more step forward . . ."

But that was where I had stopped and called out—to the One who always leads in the right direction.

We Had to Stop

— Lola M. Autry —

The rain had been coming down since dawn in northern Mississippi, when my husband, Ewart, and I drove twenty-six miles to the church where he preached. It hadn't let up by the time we were ready to head back home that night.

As we arranged our wet umbrellas in the car and buckled up I heard myself humming an old spiritual, "Angels watchin' over me . . ." My husband squinted to see the road as the headlamps became coated with muck. But we were used to flooding in our area. The swishing windshield wipers and purring motor lulled me to sleep.

"Stop!" I screamed, waking suddenly.

Ewart's foot immediately hit the brakes. Then he looked at me, astonished. "Why?" he asked.

I was as bewildered as he. "I just know we *had* to stop," I said.

We were about halfway home, somewhere near the bridge into Hickory Flat. Taking the flashlight from the glove compartment, my husband sloshed out into the two inches of water covering the road. He moved to the front of the car to see if things looked okay and shrugged his shoulders at me. With one hand on the hood, he stepped back with his right foot to wipe off the muddy headlamps. Suddenly he lost his balance and lunged forward, grabbing for the hood with both hands. He held on, looking down over his shoulder.

Less than six inches separated us from a twenty-foot-deep channel of raging water. The bridge had washed away.

GOD'S ANGELS HELP US

The angel of the Lord encamps
around those who fear him, and delivers them.
—Psalm 34:7 (NRSV)

Are they [angels] not all ministering spirits sent forth to serve,
for the sake of those who are to obtain salvation?
—Hebrews 1:14 (RSV)

Someone Parked the Car

— Dorothy Howard —

I was driving home after visiting my family for Christmas. Traffic on the two-lane road was slow but steady. A fine mist saturated the cold air, and as the temperature dropped, the highway grew slick.

Suddenly my wheels skidded and the brakes locked. The guardrail was coming up fast! I cried out, "God, help me!" The impact of the crash threw me over the seat and I blacked out.

I woke up on the floor in the backseat. A man and a boy were bent over me. "You hit a patch of ice," the man said. "A policeman saw the whole thing. He's radioing for help."

Peering out the window, I realized that my car had been moved to the opposite side of the highway and parked safely on the grass off the shoulder. *How in the world did I get over here?* Before I could ask, another car hit the same patch of ice and spun into the guardrail—at the exact spot I had. The man and his son ran to help.

When trucks arrived to sand the road, father and son

returned with the policeman. "By the way," the policeman said, "what happened to your companion?"

I looked at him quizzically: "What companion?"

"He drove the car to this spot," the officer said. "I saw him."

"We saw him too," said the father. "He crossed the lane of oncoming traffic and parked right here. But no one got out. In fact, we had to break a window to get in."

There had been no man in my car. But Someone had been with me.

The Push that Saved Me
— Kristina Seidel —

The coach complimented me on the great practice I was having at the gym. I went from one event to the next, running through gymnastics routines I wanted to master for competition.

When I got to the uneven bars I was tired and sweaty. But I was still determined to attempt the dismount I'd been practicing in the pit, a rectangle filled with foam that provided a soft landing. This time I was psyched to try it on the mats. "Dear God," I prayed as I climbed up on the bar, "please keep me safe. Amen."

Hanging by my hands, body extended, I swung once around the bar, placed my feet outside my chalked hands and snapped into the air, flipping forward—

But I'd released too early. I didn't have the height to complete a flip and land on my feet. Suddenly, in mid arc, I felt my coach push me so that the upper part of my body landed safely on the mat. The rest of me crashed down on the thin layer of carpet that covered the cement floor.

While Coach iced my back, I remembered my prayer. Why hadn't God helped me as I'd asked?

The pain was excruciating. My fall would probably keep me out of gymnastics for a while, but I realized that I could have been paralyzed if my head and neck hadn't landed on the mat. I thanked my coach for the push that had saved me.

He looked at me, puzzled. "Krissy," he said, "you flew off that bar so fast, no one had time to get anywhere near you."

The Angel of Opportunity

— Fay Angus —

On a Friday evening in November, as was my habit, I stopped by the delicatessen after work. All day I had looked forward to an end-of-week treat—fish and chips, perhaps, or a stodgy pork pie. But the evening was soaking wet with a penetrating Pacific Northwest chill.

I joined the throng of umbrellas clustered around the deli window. Standing next to me was a hunched-over figure in a thin, frayed jacket. From the peak of the cap pulled low over his forehead dripped a steady stream of rain. Every few seconds he gave a shudder, as though his bones were rattling from the cold. He looked at the food with the hypnotic stare of a most hungry man. *Poor fellow*, I thought. I wondered whether I should buy him something to eat. I checked my watch. My bus was due momentarily; another was not due for over an hour. No, I couldn't take the time to buck the crowd, either for myself or for him. I elbowed my way out and started to walk briskly to the corner.

But as is so often the case when the push of our soul leans

against the hardness of our heart, I hesitated and looked back. He was looking directly at me . . . pathetic, pleading. I spun on my heel and walked on. But only for a few paces. Again I was gripped by that overwhelming desire to look back. I knew suddenly that whether or not I missed the bus, I needed to get that man something to eat.

But he was gone. Vanished. I walked up and down the street with an urgent obsession, but I could not find him. *Was he an angel of opportunity in disguise?* I wondered miserably as I rode my bus home. If so, I had missed the opportunity.

A few years ago I had a conversation with a man who had met Mother Teresa. Touched by her messages, he asked her, "May I come with you back to India? I want to learn more of all your teachings."

"If you want to learn my teachings," she replied, "you do not have to come with me. Take the money you would spend on the air fare and give it to the poor. There! You have *all* my teachings."

Estela's Angel

— Marilyn Carlson Webber —

"You'll be interested in this," my husband said, handing me the morning paper. Indeed I was interested! There in *The Press-Enterprise* was the story of a fifty-year-old woman named Estela Vera who had lost a leg—and almost her life—after being deliberately run down by a truck on the streets of our own city of Riverside, California. But there was more to the assault than senseless violence, for this was a story of how an angel of the Lord had appeared at the precise moment when the truck was bearing down on Estela Vera. "I looked at him," the article reported her saying, "and I knew I wasn't going to die."

I myself believe firmly in angels. I believe they are present among us today, guarding us, warning us, delivering us from danger just as surely now as they did in Bible times. Over the years, I have collected a file of stories that people have told me about their encounters with these heavenly beings, and so it was particularly exciting to think that here, close at hand, was another story waiting to be told. But there was something unusual about this angel. It disturbed me that though a woman's life had been spared, this angel had not saved her from physical harm.

Estela Vera had been in the hospital for more than a month by the time I called and asked if I could come see her. Her daughter, Martha, told me I would be welcome. But then I faced the prospect of a visit with mixed emotions: Eager as I was to hear her account of her angel, I was hesitant about asking this sad woman to recall any of the circumstances of such a shocking assault. From what I'd learned in the newspaper, she'd had her fill of tragic times. She'd been raised in severe poverty. Her father was murdered when she was nine. She'd helped educate her brothers and sisters, and she herself had managed to become a registered nurse. But that career ended when a viral infection took away her hearing. Only recently she'd turned to sewing, enrolling in a professional sewing school. Then, two weeks before she graduated, came the accident.

It happened on the day before Easter. Estela went out with Martha and her son Mingo to buy dyes for her grandchildren's Easter eggs. As they drove back from a store in Riverside they saw an ice cream truck parked at the curb on Polk Avenue. The driver had been forced out of the cab by a robber, who had him in a choke hold with a knife at his throat.

Mingo and Martha leaped out and ran across the street. Mingo grabbed the assailant from behind; the man turned, slashing in fury, then jumped into the truck, turned the ignition key and gunned the motor. As Mingo grabbed on to the side of the truck, the robber stepped on the gas, and the truck shot straight across the street toward Estela, who was standing beside her car. The truck slammed into the car, shattering its hubcap spokes and crushing Estela. The man reversed the truck, ran over her again, severing one leg and nearly cutting off the other. Estela went into cardiac arrest. By the time the ambulance arrived, she'd lost seven pints of blood, and the paramedics told Martha and Mingo she probably wouldn't live to reach the emergency room. At the hospital, the doctors continued to give the family little hope. But hour after hour, then day after day, Estela rallied. The medical staff was astounded.

Even on the day I was to meet Estela in the hospital, I remained hesitant. I stood outside her room wondering what kind of a pathetic person I would find. Finally I went in.

A small woman with dark hair looked up from a hospital bed and gave me one of the warmest smiles I'd ever seen. "You're so good to come see me," she said, and I knew immediately that she meant it. Estela's daughter was at her bedside, helping with the conversation, which was a mixture of lipreading and gestures.

For a while it seemed that Estela was asking more questions about me than I was about her. Then I told her of my abiding fascination with angels and her face glowed. Obviously this was something she wanted to talk about. "But first," she said, "do you read the Bible?" I nodded that I did. "Do you know the passage in Psalm Thirty-four, 'The angel of the Lord encamps around those who fear him, and delivers them'?" (v. 7, RSV).

"Oh, yes, I do," I assured her.

"How wonderful," she said, "because that's what came into my mind just before the truck hit me." Estela took a deep breath. "That man—his face was filled with hate. He saw me and drove straight at me. It all happened so fast, I couldn't move. I just froze with terror. That's when a prayer went up from my heart and the words from the psalm shot through my mind. 'The angel of the Lord encamps . . .' "

I sat spellbound as Estela told how suddenly the form of a man appeared beside the ice cream truck, running toward her. This man was surrounded by a pink glow. He seemed to be all soft, vaporous light. His movements were graceful and fluid; his hands were extended, almost reassuringly, palms open toward her. He had the most loving eyes she'd ever seen, and the kindest smile.

As if in slow motion she saw the truck coming toward her, her daughter screaming, her son hanging on to the side of the truck, trying to stop the robber. But in the same moment she saw the man. And the love radiating from his eyes was more powerful than the hate in the eyes of her assailant. Suddenly she had no fear at all, only peace. Estela knew then that this was an angel from God.

The angel reached her a hair's-breadth before the truck did. He cradled her in his arms. She was only vaguely aware of being hit, of being put into an ambulance, of being rushed into surgery. It was like a dream. She remembered whispering the whole of Psalm 34 before she lost consciousness. *The angel of the Lord encamps . . .*

When Estela finished her story she took my hands, as if to emphasize the urgency of what she was saying. "The angel was . . . *so beautiful*," she whispered. "Somehow, without speaking, he promised me that everything would be all right. He was giving me the strength I would need to face the surgeries, to go on with life. Such caring, such peace flowed from him that I knew I would be safe."

Estela sat back, she was at ease. There was no anger in her, no bitterness toward the man who had run her down. She seemed to bask in a glow of serenity, and by the time I left her that day, I too basked in that glow. Nobody could be so close to a miracle without feeling it.

On the way home I thought about how I'd wondered why Estela's angel had not come and lifted her away from danger. Now I knew. This was a *comforting* angel. And in a way he had saved Estela. He transformed her into a person of strength, able to rise above pain and hate, truly able to forgive her attacker, and brave enough to triumph over the most terrifying of ordeals.

Then, almost out loud, I said to myself, *Angels don't always rescue people!* In Acts 27 the angel didn't save Paul from shipwreck, but it did take away his fear. In the Garden of Gethsemane, when Jesus prayed, "Father, if you are willing, take this cup from me; yet, not my will but yours be done," God did not stop the crucifixion—but "an angel from heaven appeared to him and gave him strength" (Luke 22:43, NRSV). No, a comforting angel gives succor and the courage to endure.

I see my friend Estela often since our first meeting in her hospital room. She's continuing to do the sewing she loves, making quilts and clothing for underprivileged children. And whenever I speak to groups about angels, I include the thrilling story of Estela Vera. I never get tired of telling it.

My belief in these supernatural creatures has always been firm. But today I'm even more confident that God's angels *are* among us, guiding us, protecting us and giving us comfort. Always comfort.

Nurse with a Smile

— Sue Bryson —

When my husband, Johnny, entered a hospital in Houston, Texas, two large aneurysms pressed on his heart and spinal cord. Johnny was scared and uncertain. The surgery might leave him paralyzed and he didn't want to live as an invalid. We prayed for God's guidance in this decision. Finally Johnny asked me to leave for a while so he could think.

I went to get a cup of coffee with my brother Jack, who had come with us. "Without that operation," I told him, "Johnny probably won't live out the year."

When Jack and I returned an hour later Johnny was alone in his room, smiling. "You have to meet my nurse, Shu-Lin," he said. "She has convinced me to have the operation."

Shu-Lin had assured Johnny he was in good hands, and promised to pray for him. "Not to worry," she had said. How had she given my husband confidence when the doctors and I couldn't? "You'll understand when you see her smile," Johnny said.

Jack and I met Shu-Lin later that afternoon. She was

everything Johnny had described—Asian in appearance, warm, caring and cheerful, with a radiant smile.

Johnny's sister Jane arrived to be with us for the surgery, and we went to the waiting room. Shu-Lin accompanied Johnny into surgery. It was her day off, but she said she wanted to be there. During the operation, she returned periodically to let us know how Johnny was doing. Each time she appeared, we felt relief and optimism. Finally the surgery was over, and Shu-Lin came to give us the good news even before the doctor reported to us.

Johnny spent the next five days in intensive care. Often he woke up to find Shu-Lin wiping his forehead or holding his hand. When he was out of danger, Shu-Lin came to say good-bye. "I must go now," she said. "Others need me."

The following week, Johnny was well enough to go home. We decided I should find Shu-Lin to thank her for being so kind. But when I inquired about her, the nurses on duty just looked at me. They had never heard of her. Johnny and Jack and Jane and I *knew* she had been with us. I went to the administration office, determined to locate Shu-Lin. But I was told there was no such employee.

At that moment I realized: Hospitals don't keep records of guardian angels.

A Stirring to Pray

— E. Ruth Glover —

On one of California's most beautiful days I suggested that my mother, two-year-old Jeffrey and I take a jaunt downtown. Our son, Jeffie, and I kissed my husband, Hal, goodbye and left him seated at his desk. In a few short weeks he would be graduating, and we would be leaving for the Northwest, where he had accepted a call to pastor a church.

The walk to the bus was leisurely and pleasant. Then, while we were downtown dawdling at the windows of a department store, Jeffie pulled away. Before I could reach him, he hopped-skipped-and-jumped to the curb. He paused, looked back and grinned saucily at me.

I spoke as calmly as I could, considering that my heart was in my mouth. "Come here, Jeffie."

Jeffie teetered on the edge of the curb, his blue eyes challenging mine. Just a few feet beyond him surged the downtown traffic. I stood rooted to the spot. A quick grab was impossible. The glint of glee on Jeffie's face made me feel certain that a lunge in his direction would result in his further retreat—into the unspeakable horror of the traffic beyond him.

I came up with the no-nonsense voice I reserved for serious situations: "Jeffie, get back here right now!" A look of mischief lit his face and then he whirled. He dove between the parked cars and hurled himself into the path of a city bus. The driver never saw him. Every semblance of strength left my body. I stood petrified with fear.

At what would have been the moment of impact, Jeffie was abruptly checked and spun around. It seemed incredible . . . unreal.

The traffic roared on. On unsteady legs I managed the distance to the curb, reached for my son and gathered him into my arms.

As we rode home on the bus, it seemed clear to my mother and me that Someone had come between Jeffie and that moving vehicle.

Hal met us at the door, and when he saw our ashen faces, he asked, "What happened?"

I wept as I told him how near we had come to losing our son.

"Now let me tell you what happened while you were gone," Hal said quietly.

"While I was sitting at my desk and studying, a strange stirring to prayer rose in my spirit. I couldn't understand it, and at first I tried to set it aside and go on with my work. But it was persistent."

Hal went on to tell how he had finally obeyed the inner

tug, slipped out of his chair and knelt. There he took the inexplicable burden to the Lord. Not sure of the need, Hal lifted each loved one by turn to the Throne of Grace. His intercession continued until the load lifted. Then, with peace restored, he resumed his studies.

The Invisible Finger

— Daniel Schantz —

Midnight. The warm September air surrounds me, and I am lying in bed, trying vainly to sleep. My wife Sharon is out of town, speaking at a women's retreat. I am all alone in this ancient ten-room house, my only company a squeaky fan in the far corner of the room. I am exhausted, but I can't seem to relax and fall asleep. I try reading my Bible, but after a few passages I don't have the concentration. I lay it open on the bedside table and snap off the lamp.

One o'clock. I stare at the ceiling and see specters of fear. Unpaid bills. Imminent conflicts. Regrets. Waves and waves of worry. Loneliness.

Two o'clock. Suddenly, there is a sound in the darkness, just inches from my head. It's the crinkle of paper. I stop breathing. It's my Bible! The pages are turning themselves, as if an invisible finger is nudging the pages. A chill goes through me. Another page turns. Then another. At last the pages are still.

I flip on the lamp and look around the empty room. Then

I glance at my open Bible, wondering what my mysterious visitor has selected for me to read. A passage is underlined with a ballpoint pen that I recognize as Sharon's: "It is senseless of you to work so hard from early morning until late at night, fearing you will starve to death; for God wants his loved ones to get their proper rest" (Psalm 127:2, TLB).

Two-fifteen. I flip off the lamp, lie back and pray:

Lord, thank You for my bedroom fan, a kind of Holy Ghost, Whose gentle fingers of wind reached across my room and picked a passage of truth to remind me to let You run the world.

Flutter of Tiny Wings

— Janelle Rice —

Because of lung problems, I need supplemental oxygen all the time. A device in my bathroom pumps extra oxygen into my bedroom. By using a hose extension I can move safely around the house, or even work in my garden.

One night I awoke at about 4:00 A.M., my throat bone-dry. I needed a drink of water. Thinking I could make it without the oxygen hose, I headed the short distance to the bathroom.

As I filled a glass, I found myself struggling to breathe. The heat given off by the pump made the air warm and stale. I tried to draw in deep breaths but could only manage shallow gasps. My lungs were screaming for oxygen.

I sank onto the edge of the tub. I knew I needed to get out of there, but I was too weak. *God, please help me!*

Suddenly, close to the right side of my head I felt a vibration, like the rapid fluttering of tiny wings. It seemed as though invisible fans stirred the heavy air; a cool, almost imperceptible current flowed across my mouth and nose. The slight movement of air was enough to relax my breathing. Gradually my gasps became less frantic, and I was able to make my way shakily back to the bedroom.

There was no possible source for the current of air in the bathroom. But it was unmistakably there, accompanied by the faint reassuring flutter of tiny wings. The Bible says, "He shall give his angels charge over thee" (Psalm 91:11). That doesn't necessarily mean big, stately angels. Small ones will do.

That Blue Toyota Truck

— Cheryl Toth —

Our car broke down in the middle of the West Texas desert, fifty miles from the nearest town. My kids and I tried to flag down some help, but no one stopped. Finally I sat down behind the wheel and prayed to the Lord to help us.

In time a small blue Toyota truck pulled up and an older couple stepped out. Then, to my amazement, the woman said, "We were on another highway and we heard in our prayers that someone needed our help."

The man said he was a mechanic. He looked under the hood of my car and told me that because of a malfunctioning alternator my battery was dead. "We'll take the battery to get it recharged," he said. They left us some sandwiches to eat and a red toolbox full of valuable tools to reassure me of their return.

After two hours they came back with a new battery, which the man installed. Then his wife placed her hands gently on my cheeks and said, "You'll be all right, Cheryl." She turned to my young children and added, "Michael and Janet, be good to your Mommy. See that she gets home safely to Indiana."

They got in their truck. Only after they had driven away did it occur to me: They knew my name. They knew my children's names. They knew where we were going. But we had told them none of these things.

The Man on the Rock

— Patsy Ruth Miller —

Way back in 1922, when I was in my teens and acting in silent films, I was invited by Tom Mix, one of the great Hollywood cowboys, to a barbecue on the beach at Malibu.

Malibu was then just a slim strip of sand with a few houses on it. During the party that afternoon I foolishly went swimming alone. Not long after I dived into the water, I found myself so far out that I could barely see our group. I tried to swim in, but no matter how hard I stroked, the shore grew farther away. I was caught in the beach's infamous riptide.

Salt water burned my throat, my arms felt as though they carried lead weights and I could barely kick my weary legs. "Dear God," I prayed in desperation, "help me."

At that moment I heard, "Reach up." There on a large rock was a man in a bathing suit holding out his hand. Swiftly he pulled me up beside him. When I could breathe evenly, he said, "You can make it now. Head for the piling that sea gull is on."

It seemed the wrong direction, but I did as he said. As I

swam away, I turned around briefly and he raised his hand. The next time I looked he was gone.

At last I made it back to shore and trudged up to the barbecue. Someone asked where I'd been. Exhausted, I replied, "I took a swim out to the rock."

"What rock?" Tom Mix asked. "There's no rock out there." I looked out to sea. Tom was right. I could not find the rock I'd been on. And yet . . .

Today I'm in my eighties. Throughout my long life with all its crosscurrents and contrary tides, I've known there *is* a rock. And a man holding out his hand to me.

GOD'S PRESENCE
CHANGES US

In your presence there is fullness of joy. . . .
—Psalm 16:11 (NRSV)

"And lo, I am with you always, to the close of the age."
—Matthew 28:20 (RSV)

The Timeless Moment
— Elaine St. Johns —

The habit of prayer—even on those days when your words seem more mechanical than meaningful—is a way of preparing yourself to expect, and receive, God's help when the unexpected happens. I found that out in a sudden, drastic moment when I had no time to pray . . .

It does not take long for a car to go over a cliff. One instant the convertible I was riding in was right side up on the night-black, mountainous Topanga Canyon Road between the bright lights of the San Fernando Valley and the beach houses on the Pacific Ocean. The next instant it was upside down in a tangle of scrub and brush far below. And I was pinned under the car, fully conscious, paralyzed from the neck down.

It should have been one of the darkest moments of my life.

But it wasn't.

For between that one instant and the next, I had actually felt God's presence. It came as an inner voice repeating three times the beautiful promise, "Lo, I am with you always"

(Matthew 28:20). Simultaneously, I entered into a timeless moment where the love of God was a substance—comforting, warm, light-bright, peace-filled, enveloping.

The moment passed, but the peace, His peace, remained.

Subsequent events unfolded rapidly. I smelled gas fumes. I called to my driver-companion—he had been thrown clear and was confused but unhurt—to turn off the ignition. All at once, although I had no medical competence, I knew my neck was "broken." I asked my companion to pull me out from the wreckage firmly, steadily, holding my feet. As he did so, the spinal cord was released from pressure. Feeling returned. (Later we were told how damaging this might have been.)

Then a car came along the lonely road and stopped; two men carried me carefully up the cliff, drove me to a hospital and disappeared. Again, potentially dangerous consequences. Yet it could have been hours before we were discovered, and since we were in an area where a dispute about ambulance service was going on, even more hours might have elapsed before help arrived.

At the hospital, the doctors waited for me to go into shock. I never did. Nor did I lose my calm during the medical crises and emergencies of the ensuing weeks.

All this, the hospital staff decided, was "lucky." I knew it wasn't. It was the result of one great miracle, that moment in which I experienced God's love.

In my prayers and Bible studies, I had sometimes felt discouraged about my capacity to receive Christ's Word "in an honest and good heart, and bring forth fruit with patience"

(Luke 8:15, RSV). Too often, it seemed that the fruit of my efforts to improve my spiritual practice was to be patience alone.

Then, in a moment of extremity, when I could do nothing of myself, when I had no time to struggle or pray or even think, the fruit appeared in my readiness to receive His instant grace: "Lo, I am with you alway."

And He was.

"It Will Be All Right"

— Frances O. Jansen —

The excruciating pain in my back had been getting worse for months. Diathermy treatments, massage, bed rest and painkillers had barely eased my suffering.

Surgery terrified me. I tried to fall back on my faith in God and kept repeating the platitudes I had heard all my life: "Have faith—God never puts burdens on you heavier than you can bear." Nothing helped.

My husband felt helpless. I was a member of a Protestant church. He was a "fallen-away" who had not prayed since he was a boy. On one of the days when I was having an especially difficult time, Elmer asked me, "Where's that Supreme Being you're always praying to? Why doesn't He help you now?"

All I could do was answer weakly, "There's a reason for this."

That night I sank into despair. Silently I cried out to the Lord, demanding to know, *Why me, God? What is this plague You have sent me?*

About midnight, sleep took over. What happened next I

could not share with anyone, not even my husband, lest people think I had gone over the edge.

I slept facing the hallway, where a small light burned during the night. The bedroom door was open. Suddenly I opened my eyes, and there in the doorway—for just a second or two—stood Jesus, His right hand outstretched. And just before He disappeared from view, he said, "It will be all right." His white robe seemed to leave a bright glow for another brief instant.

I glanced at the clock on the dresser. The lighted dial read 2:43 A.M. I turned my head toward my husband and heard only his gentle snore.

An indescribable peace entered my body. The pain was still there, but somehow it didn't matter. Taking my cane, I made my way into the hallway, half expecting to see Jesus still there.

The words echoed in my head: *It will be all right.* I had not been dreaming. I went into the bathroom and stared into the mirror. There was a strange look in my eyes, a stare of awe, of amazement, of delight. I felt wonderful!

The next day I found out *why* Jesus had come. The day began like most. I eased my aching body out of bed. Yet I felt so confident that I decided to get dressed. As I put my left leg into my girdle, I screamed in agony, and Elmer came running.

An ambulance took me to the hospital. Tests showed a herniated disk in the lower back. My doctor and several experts agreed that I could heal without surgery. I spent thirty days in traction.

Each day as I awoke I heard in my mind: *It will be all right.* It was. On the thirty-first day I was able to get out of bed. The next day I went home and into a rented hospital bed, then to a wheelchair, crutches, and finally a cane. I wore a back-support girdle and a back brace. I still wear the girdle daily, and occasionally I have to use the back brace.

During the following years several tragedies touched my life. "How can you be so strong?" a friend asked. It would have been a perfect time to tell her that Jesus had appeared to me, sent by God to give me the assurance that has carried me through misfortune and good times alike. But I held back for fear of what she and others might think.

Now I am seventy-eight years old. It's been more than twenty years since Jesus appeared to me. Recently in church a soloist sang the hymn "Blessed Assurance, Jesus Is Mine!" and I felt my message from God should no longer be a secret.

I have never questioned why God sent his Son to visit me that night. I truly believe I would not have been able to carry the burden without the optimistic attitude he furnished me. By telling me, "It will be all right," Jesus helped me bear the load.

Visitation

— John Sherrill —

I was in an upbeat mood that morning in 1959, striding uptown for a follow-up visit at my doctor's. I'd been coming to Daniel Catlin's office every month since an operation two years earlier for melanoma, a particularly vicious form of cancer. Always before it was the same: The surgeon's skilled fingers running down my neck, the pat on the back. "See you in a month."

But not that day. This time Dr. Catlin's fingers stopped, prodded, worked a long time. He shook his head. When I left I was scheduled for surgery at New York's Memorial Hospital the following day.

What a difference in a spring morning! I walked back down the same street in the same sunshine, but now a cold, light-headed fear walked with me. I was not expected to live beyond three months.

Tib and I were having coffee the next morning after a sleepless night when the telephone rang. It was our neighbor, Catherine Marshall LeSourd. "John," she said, "could you and

Tib drive over? I've heard the news and there's something I've got to ask you." Catherine met us at the door dressed in a housecoat, wearing neither makeup nor smile. She led us into the family room, shut the door and, without polite talk, began.

"First of all I want to say that I know it's presumptuous to ask you about your religious life. I have no right to assume that it lacks anything."

I looked at Tib. She sat still as a rock.

"John," said Catherine, "do you believe that Jesus was God?"

It was the last question I'd expected. I'd supposed she'd have something to say about God's power to heal, or the crisis I faced. But she'd put the question to me, so I considered it. Tib and I were Christians, certainly, in the sense that we attended various churches off and on, and sent our three children to Sunday school. Still, I had never come to grips with this very question: Was Jesus of Nazareth in fact God? And now, when I tried to do so, there were mountains of logic in the way. I started to map them for Catherine, but she stopped me.

"You're trying to arrive at faith through your mind, John," she said. "It simply can't be done that way. It's one of the peculiarities of Christianity," she went on, "that you have to do something you *don't* understand before you can understand. And it's this I'm hoping for you today—that without knowing why, against all logic, you say yes to Christ."

There was silence in the room and I had a sudden desire to do precisely what Catherine was suggesting. Yet I had reservations. The biggest of all, I stated frankly: It didn't seem right to shy away from Christ all these years and then come running when I had my back to the wall.

"John," said Catherine almost in a whisper, "that's pride. You want to come to God *your* way. As you will. When you will. Maybe God wants you now, without a shred to recommend you."

We talked for perhaps a half hour more. When Tib and I left, I still had not brought myself to take the step that was apparently all-crucial. A few moments later, however, as we drove past a telephone pole on Millwood Road, a pole that I can point out to this day, I turned to Tib.

"What do they call it? A leap of faith? All right, I'm going to make the leap: I believe that Jesus was God."

It was a cold-blooded laying down of my sense of what was logical, quite without emotional conviction. And with it went something that was essentially "me." All the bundle of self-consciousness that we call our ego seemed to dissolve in this decision. It was amazing how much it hurt. But when this thing was dead and quiet finally, and I had blurted out my simple statement of belief, there was room for something new and altogether mysterious.

Millwood Road was the route to St. Mark's Episcopal Church in Mount Kisco, N.Y., where Tib and I had attended services for the past several months. We headed there now. The gray stone church offered solidity, permanence. And though the rector, Marc Hall, a retired Navy officer, was new to the priesthood, to a Christian five minutes old he was a veteran of the faith.

To our relief Marc was in. He stood up, unwinding his angular frame from behind his desk, and extended a huge hand. I told him I was entering Memorial Hospital that afternoon for surgery the next day and asked if the church had prayers for a situation like mine.

Marc reached for *The Book of Common Prayer*. "I know there are . . ." As he thumbed the pages, I had the sense that he felt as shy hearing my request as I'd been in making it. "Ah, here we are. Shall we go into the chapel?"

Midmorning light streamed through Tiffany windows into the Chapel of the Resurrection. Holding the prayer book, Marc stepped behind the Communion rail while Tib and I knelt before him on the needlepoint cushion.

Marc plunged into the prayer. Certain words stood out: "I lay my hand upon thee . . . beseeching the mercy of our Lord Jesus Christ . . ." Marc hesitated, then I felt one of those big hands on my head. "That all thy pain and sickness of body being put to flight, the blessing of health may be restored unto thee."

At that moment I felt a sudden rush of heat. Marc's hand was burning! The heat coursed down the side of my head and settled in my neck just where the surgeon's fingers had stopped the day before. Marc finished the prayer in a choked voice. I began to cry. So did Tib. The heat in Marc's hand burned, scorched, singeing my neck.

I heard Marc close the book. Tib and I stood up. The three of us stood blinking at each other, stunned, tearful, awed, embarrassed. Baffled by what had taken place. Quite unready to talk about it.

Four hours later Tib accompanied me as I checked into Memorial Hospital. That evening Dr. Catlin stopped by my bedside, trailed by half a dozen young physicians. "Melanoma," he told them, looking at his chart. He ran his free hand down the side of my neck. A puzzled look spread across his face. He put down his chart and felt my neck now with both hands, pursed his lips, felt again. With the young doctors in tow, he retreated to the hall where I heard, ". . . better go in anyhow."

What was happening? And why was I curiously uninterested? It was as if in some secret and undefined part of myself I knew that no matter how this operation turned out, it was only an inconvenience in an existence that was new and strange and quite independent of surgeons and hospitals, illness and recovery.

Early the next morning orderlies wheeled me into the operating room. I remember the bright lights overhead, and the green-masked face of Dr. Catlin looking down at me.

It seemed only an instant later that I was awake again, in a room I had never seen before. It was dark outside the window—but I'd gone into the operating room at eight in the morning. Why had it taken so long? Plastic tubes protruded from both sides of my chest, and from a hole in my throat. I could hear machines gurgling. And there was pain. The worst I had ever known.

In the morning I woke up in yet another room. The tubes were still in my chest and throat, machines still bubbled away. But there was wonderful news. Dr. Catlin leaned over the bed:

"You're doing fine. There was some trouble on the operating table. Your lungs collapsed. Tracheotomy. The tumor in your neck, though ..." The same puzzled look as when he'd spoken to the young doctors. "I didn't find it. Just a little dried-up pea, more like a cinder."

For the rest of that day I lay there in pain, aware of an occasional visit from Tib or the doctor, trying to take in the fact that a healing miracle could take place through a prayer in a suburban church.

That night I became more aware of the two other patients in the room. One, an older man, coughed almost constantly. The other, a teenager just down from Recovery, moaned in pain. Despite my embryonic faith I tried praying for them, but the coughing and the moans continued.

In the middle of the night I was awake suddenly. Fully awake. A dim yellow light came in from the hall; a nurse passed the door on rubber-soled shoes. Both of my roommates were restless.

Then a light came through the outer wall of the hospital. It was simply there, as abruptly as I'd awakened. It was different from the light coming through the door, warmer, yet more intense, with—indescribably—a center of awareness. I was awed, but not at all afraid.

"Christ?" I said.

The light moved. Rather, it was immediately closer to me. I thought for a moment that the pain beneath my bandages was going away, but it did not. Something had changed, though. Despite the pain, I felt as if I were bursting with health.

My roommates were still tossing, still coughing and groaning. "Christ," I said, "would You help that boy?" The light did not leave me, but in some strange way it was also now at the bedside of the teenager. A little "Ohhh . . ." came from him and he was silent.

"And my other friend?" The light was instantly centered on the bed of the old man who was in the midst of another coughing spasm. The coughing stopped.

And the light was gone.

I lifted my head from the pillow and searched the room but there was only the yellow light from the hall. A car honked outside in the night. The machines behind my bed gurgled. Everything was as it had been. Except that, lying in a bed in Memorial Hospital, with bandages around my neck and chest, with pain slicing through me, I was filled with a sense of well-being such as I had never known. I cried for a long time, out of joy.

I stayed awake until dawn. All the while my two roommates slept quietly.

I was out of the hospital a full week earlier than expected, so rapidly did my body mend. For several days afterward I tried to tell Tib about the encounter in the hospital, but every time I opened my mouth I felt tears well up. I knew that if I said one word I'd be weeping like a child. It was only when I decided that Tib would have to know about the experience, tears or no, that I managed to get it out.

"Do you think it was a dream?" I asked.

"I don't believe a dream could affect you this way."

"Neither do I."

Before that experience, I had been given three months to live. Since that day, to my surprise, a reality far more engrossing than physical survival has occupied my mind: the reality of Jesus Christ, whose light has shaped my life ever since—as vivid, mysterious and joy-filled today as it was in that predawn hour thirty-five years ago.

The Figure in the Fire
— Bud Ward —

If I had not obeyed that strange impulse to take the other road that day, my whole life would be different.

At noon on Friday, December 5, 1980, in our little town of Deptford in southern New Jersey, I had picked up my wife Joan at work and we were driving home for lunch. It was a bright, crisp day, and for a moment the sun had lifted my gloomy spirits. They needed lifting; the past year had been the worst of my forty-nine.

My troubles began when a contractor who was to remodel our house absconded with our money, leaving the house unfinished. Not long after that, I suffered a stroke that left me partially paralyzed and with slurred, halting speech. I carried an emergency medical card that read: "APHASIA. Stroke, limited walking, speech problems. My doctor is . . ."

As a result, I was unable to continue my freelance photography for eleven months, until September, when I convinced my doctor to allow me to work on a limited basis.

I did not normally pick Joan up for lunch, but on that

December day I was feeling particularly gloomy, wondering why God had let so many bad things happen to me, and I thought lunch with Joan would lift my spirits.

Driving the van on Fox Run Road, I approached the street where I would normally turn right; but I had a sudden, strong urge to turn left. So I did.

"Bud, where are you going?" Joan asked. "You know I only have an hour for lunch."

I shook my head. "Don't . . . know," I said. And I didn't. All I knew was that I'd had the strong urge to turn left, and I'd done it. Suddenly above the houses ahead surged a huge pillar of black smoke.

"Oh . . . oh, I guess that's where I'm going," I muttered. Until my stroke I had also been the photographer for the Deptford Township Fire District. Suddenly I felt I was back on the job again.

Twisting the wheel with my good arm, I turned onto a narrow dirt road leading to the smoke.

An ancient shed on the old Tarpy farm was burning furiously. The shed had been locked, unused for years. Now it was enveloped in fire. Fed by the dry wood, flames were snapping and crackling and leaping upward in bright orange sheets; deep pitch-colored smoke was boiling heavenward.

The fire department hadn't arrived yet and no one else was there. I pulled up across the road and stopped. "Bud!" Joan wailed with irritation. "We don't have time for this."

Disregarding her, and breathing heavily, I fumbled for my 35-mm camera behind the seat. "Got . . . to . . . take . . .

shots." I struggled to get the words out as I worked myself out of the van and stood on the roadside. I focused my viewfinder on the shed. The fire would consume it soon, no great loss or danger to other buildings, but the intensity of the fire was spectacular and I wanted to capture it.

With the Minolta to my eye, I began clicking off shots.

Click. Flames roared up through a tall tree next to the building.

Click . . . click. Flames formed a ring around the shed.

Click. The two shed doors parted and slowly opened toward me. Evidently their locked hasp had separated.

Click. A sudden, quick sensation—the kind a photographer gets in his gut when he senses he has caught exactly the right shot.

Click . . . click. Six, seven pictures.

By now the fire engine had arrived. I turned back to the van.

"Bud," complained Joan, "we don't have much time left to go home for lunch."

"Sorry . . . hon. How . . . 'bout . . . eating out?"

We pulled into a drive-through fastfood place, got hamburgers and milkshakes, and then parked in the nearby K-Mart lot.

Because the professional lab I deal with does not process slide film, I decided to drop the roll of film off at K-Mart after we ate.

The next day I felt better than I had in months; the paralysis seemed to be leaving my body. I walked and moved with a limberness I hadn't felt since before the stroke. *A temporary remission*, I thought to myself, and I was grateful for it.

Two days later I walked into the kitchen where Joan was preparing breakfast for the children.

"Honey, I really feel good today," I said. "Maybe after work I'll get Chris to help me put up a few sheets of plaster-board."

Joan looked up from the stove, spatula frozen in midair, her eyes wide, then she started crying. I rushed over and put my arms around her. "Honey, what's wrong?"

She stifled a sob and looked at me through brimming eyes. "Nothing's wrong, Bud. But you're talking normally. I haven't heard that voice in almost a year!"

What's going on? I wondered. I phoned my doctor.

"Don't get excited, Bud," he soothed. "It's something we can't explain, but it's probably temporary. Things like this sometimes come and go."

The day the slides came back, I set up the slide projector and screen in the living room. Our three children, Chris, aged fourteen, Heather, nine, and Holly, eight, were in their rooms doing homework. Joan and I settled on the sofa. *Clish* went the slide mechanism. The burning shed leaped to life on the screen.

Clish. I could almost feel the heat. *Strange,* I thought, *I was only thirty feet away from the flames, yet I never even felt warm.*

Clish. Odd, how that ring of fire went around the shed in such a perfect circle.

Clish. I could see that the limbs on the tree were burning. "Oh, look," said Joan, "there's a bird's nest up in that tree."

Clish. The fifth slide; nothing much different from the others. Only the shed doors seemed to be open wider.

Heather walked into the living room. "Going to make a peanut-butter sandwich, Mom," she said. As she passed, she glanced at the screen. "Daddy," she asked, "why is Jesus standing in the fire?" She walked on into the kitchen.

I studied the screen. I could hear Joan's breath catch. We hadn't noticed it at first, but in the doorway was a figure, a figure with long hair and a robe.

We stared at it. Once more I got the feeling, that same strange feeling I'd experienced when I took that shot.

I called Chris and Holly into the living room.

"Do you see anything special in that picture?" I asked.

"Sure," said Holly, "there's Jesus standing in the doorway."

"I can't believe it!" Joan gasped.

There was no such figure in the sixth and seventh slides.

We didn't talk much about the fifth slide as I put the projector away. But I couldn't sleep that night. What was it all about?

A few days later I took the slides down to the firehouse. "Hey, Bud," exclaimed one of my friends as I walked into the engine house carrying the projector and screen, "you're moving around like nobody's business. What's up?"

"Just thought you fellows would like to see some slides of that fire on the Tarpy farm last week," I said.

I set the projector on automatic so it would present the seven slides in sequence. *Clish, clish, clish, clish.* Then the fifth slide flashed on the screen.

The room hushed. Someone in the group crossed himself. Then all the guys exploded with exclamations and questions. One of them even wanted to buy the slide then and there.

They had all seen what my kids had seen.

I took the slides home, projected the fifth slide on the screen again, and sat there in the living room studying it, mulling it over. *What was it?* I wondered. *What had happened when I took it?*

To get more reactions, I showed the set to other groups in the area. I made no claims for the fifth slide, but let people judge for themselves. The reactions were the same. People were touched, some fell to their knees and prayed when slide number five appeared. One woman called the local newspaper about it.

Word traveled fast, and soon everyone seemed to know about it. As summer blossomed, people from everywhere streamed into Deptford to see the remains of the shed. Amazingly, its skeleton, charred, was still standing. And the tree next to it, the tree that had been in flames, was blooming with fresh, green leaves. And the bird's nest was still there, its dried grass and twigs still intact.

As news of slide number five spread, more and more people wanted to see it. It was featured in magazines and on nationwide television. People reacted to it in a variety of ways. Some saw a little girl in the picture, standing in front of Christ. Others pointed to a lamb on His shoulder. "It was a sign," many said. Some claimed it presaged Christ's Second Coming. Others said it was God's way of helping people return to Him.

I pondered these questions: Was the image people saw just a chance happening? Did people "see" what they wanted to see? Often before people had shown me pictures of cloud formations, urging me to see Jesus or other images in the whorls and shadows.

Eventually I came to the conclusion that only God really knew what was in that doorway and why it was there. As for me, I did not need to see an image of Christ in a photo of a burning building to support my faith. I already believed in Him implicitly, knowing that He is with us all the time. After all, it was He who said: "Where two or three are gathered in my name, there am I in the midst of them" (Matthew 18:20, RSV).

One day someone told me, "Bud, I'd advise you to do just what you've been doing. Go out and show these slides to people, telling them that what they see is up to them. Then tell them about your healing and let them decide the meaning of that one slide."

And so that is what I am doing.

For no matter what it was that produced that image in slide number five, there is one incontrovertible fact; I am healed of my stroke. I feel very much like the man healed of blindness by Jesus, who, when questioned by doubting Pharisees, replied: ". . . one thing I know, that though I was blind, now I see" (John 9:25, RSV).

Editor's note: Bud's healing has been complete and permanent. The name of the road on which the burning building stood is Good Intent. And many years ago the town of Deptford was called Bethlehem.

A Man with a View

— William Wachter —

My wife, Ferne, and I stood in front of the small, thirty-room hotel that summer morning in 1954, so taken by its potential that we didn't see the drawbacks. The Alta Mira was already a hundred years old and looked it, with its peeling beige stucco faìade, its three acres of weeds, its too-steep driveway and limited parking. "Just think, Ferne," I said, "what this place will be like with a little work."

I said the words while looking out over the waterside village of Sausalito and farther out over San Francisco Bay. It was the view that grabbed my attention. If caution did creep into my thinking, it was my age. At fifty-six I should have been thinking about retirement, not about refurbishing some run-down old hotel.

But I took Ferne's elbow and steered her up the hotel's rickety steps, exclaiming about the terrace I would build here someday. My terrace would be attached to a first-class hotel, like the places I had known in my childhood. Known *about*, that is. When I was a youngster, my family rarely visited such establishments. My father was a glazier in Berlin; men who installed windows for a living didn't stay in fancy hotels.

Ferne and I picked our way through the lobby. I could tell why its owners were anxious to sell. The lobby was dark; tiny windows defied you to enjoy the view. From somewhere in the building came gurgling and knocking sounds as water struggled to negotiate ancient pipes. Few people wanted to stay in this bathroom-down-the-hall place.

"But we'd make a go of it, Ferne. We'd knock down the walls, open up the view. Thousands of people would stream up here. Thousands."

Whatever I decided to do, Ferne said, she was with me. We drove back to the Fairmont Hotel in San Francisco, where I was catering manager and where friends had told me about the Alta Mira. "The hotel's a bargain, Bill. With your experience, you could make something out of it."

Experience I had, all right; I'd earned it through turning my back on an old European tradition. In the ordinary course of things at the turn of the century when I was born, a dutiful son in Germany was supposed to follow his father into the family business. But as I grew up I dreamed of going into hotel management, where I could work with people instead of with a putty knife. My father slapped his trousers leg and looked away when he heard this news. But eventually he let me go. I completed a fifteen-year apprenticeship, beginning with the Adlon Hotel in Berlin, and in time managed every phase of some of the finest hotels in Europe and America.

Now at last I was about to put these decades of experience

to work with a hotel of my own. Ferne and I and two partners bought the Alta Mira for $100,000. Already I was sketching plans for my terrace, where people could eat outdoors under umbrellas during the day and by candlelight at night.

But those dreams seemed unattainable. One of my partners died shortly after we acquired the hotel. I bought out his interest, and there went the money for the plumbing system. The occasional guest who struggled up the hill didn't appreciate being awakened at 4:00 A.M. by clanging pipes. "I wouldn't stay in this boiler shop another night if it were *you* paying *me* for the room!" one man said as he made his escape.

And in trying to keep the kitchen open we put our purchases on the cuff. One morning I came into the dim lobby and was pleased to see six gentlemen waiting there. "Customers!" I whispered to Ferne as I stepped behind the front desk.

"Look again, Bill," Ferne said. "Those are our suppliers wanting their money." Day after day the same purveyors waited in the lobby, bills in hand. We paid what we could.

After a year of limping along like this my other partner wanted out. With the very last of our resources we bought the final interest. The place was ours now, but what good was that? More months passed with less and less money for cleaning up the grounds and upgrading the kitchen. We had exhausted our funds and the patience of our creditors.

"Ferne, my dear, there is no hope left," I said one night in the fall of 1958, after four years of struggle. "You might as well pack our things."

Ferne agreed. I went down to the front desk from our

apartment in the hotel to close the accounts of our two guests. Now and then I stopped to doodle on the plans for the terrace that would never come to pass. At eleven o'clock I decided to take a walk, the last ever as a hotel owner.

In the dark I headed up the path toward the rear of the grounds. Then, as I was ambling along, someone began speaking to me. The quiet voice seemed to come from inside the bushes. I looked, but couldn't see a soul, so I started walking again.

There. Again! I made out the words now: "If you follow me, I can help."

Who would be out this late, and why wasn't he showing his face? "Who's there?" I whispered. Then, more loudly, "Show yourself! I'm not going to talk to anyone who's hiding." Nothing.

I took another step forward, searching. Then the voice, again: "If you follow Me, I can help you."

This time I began to suspect. "God?" I whispered.

What should I do? "Lord?" I said, using the name Ferne sometimes used. Ferne was the one who went to church, not I. "Lord?" my voice trembled. Nothing more.

I ran back to the hotel and stumbled upstairs and opened the door, calling, "Ferne!" The light in our bedroom went on immediately. Half-packed suitcases sat on their baggage racks. "Something's happened."

I told my wife that maybe, just maybe, I had heard God speak. Actual words. About following and helping. Ferne was nodding her head up and down, saying yes, yes, even when I went on to put it more strongly: "I've met the Lord, my dear!"

The light of morning didn't quell our excitement even in the face of the same empty breakfast tables. That noon we unpacked our bags.

Over the next few days I occasionally wandered to the back of the property, where I'd met Him. What did God mean when He said He'd help? And what was the right and honorable thing to do about our debts when we had no money? These weren't exactly musings—it was more like I was talking to God, asking questions. And amazingly, it also seemed I was getting answers.

The first thing I thought the Lord told me to do was to call each of the purveyors who had been sitting in our lobby. I was to tell them I still had no money but appreciated their patience and that if I prospered they would be our suppliers for as long as I owned the hotel. Sounded like stall talk to me, but I followed Him.

Next morning there was not one bill collector waiting in the lobby.

On the third day a gentleman came to the front desk. He was not one of the purveyors, but I figured he must have been from some other creditor because he said he wanted to talk about money. I barely looked up. What more could I say to these bill collectors? "You are wasting your time, sir. I have no money."

"Banks are in the business of lending money," the man said.

"That doesn't do me any good. I have no credit."

"I think we can work something out through an insurance policy."

Slowly I began to pay attention. This man was selling life insurance. He told me he had convinced the local bank that under special circumstances the Alta Mira deserved a loan, even now. All the ingredients for success were there except capital and time. Capital, for improvements. And time, for my top experience to pay off. That's where insurance came in. The bank would lend me money for improvements; the hotel would take out a policy on my life, with the bank as beneficiary; if I died early, before the bank could be repaid from profits at the hotel, the loan would be repaid from death benefits.

One week later the bank president called me and said, "Mr. Wachter, we have the privilege of offering you a loan for one hundred thousand dollars."

Ferne and I were singing with joy. We began putting our new capital to work, asking for God's guidance at each step. First we were to pay off the banker and fishmonger and butcher and greengrocer. Then bit by bit we were to landscape, and get rid of those thumping pipes.

Most exciting of all was the day we hired the contractor to start work on the terrace. I'd been right. That terrace wasn't even finished before people started flocking in. News passed by word of mouth that the Alta Mira had a wonderful outdoor area with umbrellas and flowers and a terrific view. Before we knew it we were swamped. We had to call the contractor again with plans for expanding the terrace. With the money that now started to flow through our books we refurbished the hotel itself, three rooms at a time, each with its own bath. All of the suppliers who had kept faith with us flourished too.

Nearly thirty-four years have passed since I heard the voice on our hotel grounds. Our hotel is so successful that we get dozens of offers every year to buy us out.

But at ninety-three, where would I go and what would I do? Our church and our staff and customers are our very lives. Ferne and I thank God for this by making every effort to follow Him. Each morning over coffee we read the Bible and pray for individuals among the fifty-member hotel staff. And we pray for our guests, those who come back every year and those who are about to become our friends. Above all we thank God for the privilege of following Him in these times when every day brings some new risk.

It's interesting how, when I was twenty, my father became upset when I did not follow him down the safe and known way. Years later my heavenly Father also told me to follow Him. But He added the words which have let me see risk as adventure: "Follow Me," He said, "and I will help you."

Oh, to Have a Friend

— Helen Grace Lescheid —

Forty years ago as a lonely immigrant girl in Canada, I had an experience so hard to describe that it took me many years even to try. Yet the story needs to be told, for it points up how intimately God knows His children.

That October day in 1952 as I listened to the lunchtime chatter in my high school homeroom, the ache in my throat made it hard to swallow my meal of dark rye bread. *Won't I ever belong?*

I was fifteen. Two years earlier I'd entered Lord Tweedsmuir High in Surrey, British Columbia, a frightened newcomer from Germany. Shy and awkward anyway, I'd been too ashamed of my limited English to reply when someone spoke to me.

As the months went by my English improved but my sense of belonging did not. Everything about me was different from these outgoing Canadian girls—my accent, my hand-me-down clothes, my thick blond braids (too beautiful to cut, my mother said when I pleaded that all the other girls wore their

hair short), even the lunch I brought from home. My classmates brought sandwiches on thin-sliced white bread; I had
thick black rye and jam. I was the odd one, the outsider. In
two years I'd made not a single friend.

I stuffed my uneaten lunch back inside my desk and fled
from the happy babble of the classroom. Through crowded
halls I pushed my way to the library. Books at least were my
friends . . . but not that day. As I glanced up from reading, I
saw through the window an ordinary scene. Two girls sat on
the grass, heads together, talking. Such longing rose inside me
I knew I was going to cry. Oh, to have a friend—just one
friend with whom I could sit and talk that way!

I escaped from the library and dodged into the bathroom,
where I could lock the door and let the tears come. "Lord
Jesus, I'm so lonely!" To talk to Jesus was natural to me; I'd
been taught that He cared for each of us personally. I'd gaze
at paintings of Him, thinking how friendly He looked, how
I'd have told Him anything if I'd lived back then.

After school I stood as usual at the bus stop on the fringe
of a knot of schoolmates. One of the girls turned to me.
"Helen, are you going to the school dance on Friday?" I shook
my head no. "Why don't you come?" she coaxed.

I shut my eyes against a memory. . . . At the last dance I'd
stood on the sidelines for what seemed hours. At last a boy
walked up to me—but what he did was yank one of my braids.
Everyone had laughed. No, I'd never put myself through that
again! The girl beside me fell silent, then turned back to the
others.

I mounted the big yellow bus and scanned it for a seat by the window, where I could keep from meeting people's eyes. But the window seats were taken. I slumped down beside a girl who smiled at me. *She's friendly.* I thought. *I'd like to say something friendly to her.* I was too tongue-tied. Throughout the half-hour ride I said not a word.

Close to tears again, I stumbled off the bus and hurried into the old farmhouse. As usual our rented house was empty. Mother, who'd been widowed in World War II, worked up to ten hours in the vegetable fields each day to support herself and us four children. Come to think of it, my younger sisters and brother seemed to have no trouble making friends in our new country. They were probably off playing with the neighbor's kids at this very moment. It was me—something was terribly wrong with me.

Dropping my books on the kitchen table, I ran into the bedroom, slammed the door shut and fell across the bed. My body, so flat and long and lanky, shook with sobs.

I sat up abruptly. Someone else was in the room! Hastily wiping my eyes I looked around. Nobody. But—someone was here. I could feel it.

Not someone . . . Someone. There was an aura in that little room I could almost touch. Love such as I'd never felt before filled the space all around me. "Jesus," I whispered, "is that You?"

He answered, not with an audible voice, but with a love so tangible I felt hugged. Although I saw nothing physical, an image burned itself into my mind: a friendly face with smiling eyes, so vivid that even today forty years later I see them still. Eyes that danced . . . "You know what? I *like* you! You're my special friend!"

As I sat there on my bed, the glorious, gracious words kept coming: "Have you forgotten that you belong to Me? I will never leave you or forsake you. I'm here with you now and will always be with you. Don't be ashamed! I love you just as you are."

For a long time I sat there basking in love beyond my conceiving, hearing those words of unconditional acceptance. When my family came home they found me humming as I prepared supper.

The next morning I opened my eyes to find the joyful Presence still filling the room, as though He'd waited for me to wake up so we could start the day together. When I boarded the yellow bus He did too.

During class it was as though He were standing beside my desk. We did math problems together. We wrote essays together. Even in gym class, which I'd always dreaded, I could feel Him running beside me.

At lunch break that day one of my classmates asked me if I would help her with a problem. She hadn't understood the teacher and felt sure I had. Wondering why she'd singled me out, yet thrilled that somebody had, I slid over and made room for her at my desk—not even trying to hide my chunk of bread.

Later at the bus stop I stood with the familiar cluster of teens. My Friend whispered, "Aren't they a great bunch of kids? I also love them dearly." I turned to stare at them with new appreciation. Friendly eyes met mine. Later that week some girls invited me to join the glee club and I eagerly accepted.

The fact that my peers now *wanted* to be with me never ceased to amaze me. One day one of my sisters hinted at the reason. "Helen, what's happened to you? You're always so happy now!" I looked at her in surprise. True, I was supremely happy, but I hadn't been aware it showed.

For three glorious months my Friend and I walked in this indescribable companionship. I had never felt so completely believed in and understood. He was always smiling at me, a big smile of delight and approval, and it was impossible not to smile back at the world around me. Every morning when I got up He was there. All day He walked beside me. In the evening my last awareness was of Him.

Then one dreadful morning I awoke to an empty room. The joyful Presence was gone. Panic seized me. "Jesus!" I cried. Silence. I must have sinned in some terrible way. Frantically I searched my conscience. I confessed every sin I could recall and begged Him to forgive my unknown ones. But the almost palpable sense of His presence did not return.

Grief-stricken, I opened my Bible. Where were those words Jesus had spoken to me three months before, right in this room? I found them in the 13th chapter of Hebrews: "He hath said, 'I will never leave thee, nor forsake thee.'"

I saw the words, I believed the words. But I did not *feel* them—not the way I had before. Slowly I repeated the words, "I will *never* leave thee, nor forsake thee."

"Jesus, did you say *never* so that I might know today that You are still with me even though I don't feel You?" I whispered. This glimmer of hope in time became a growing reality: No matter how I feel, Jesus is always with me. His love and acceptance are a fact independent of my moods and feelings.

It was only much later that I understood the double gift Jesus gave to a clumsy immigrant girl. He came as a tangible Presence to assure me of my value in His sight, and to show me the value of friendship. Then He withdrew this special feeling. "You will find Me in My written Word," He seemed to be saying, "and in so many different ways." He stepped a little distance back, to make room for faith and character to grow. Isn't that what a best friend would do?

God's Love Assures Us of Life After Death

Unto God the Lord belong the issues from death.
—Psalm 68:20

Our Lord Jesus Christ, who died for us, that,
whether we wake or sleep, we should live together with him.
Wherefore comfort yourselves. . . .
—I Thessalonians 5:9)11

I'll Meet Them Again

— Norman Vincent Peale —

My father, who died at eighty-five after a distinguished career as a physician and minister, had struggled against a very real fear of death. But after his funeral, my stepmother dreamed that he came to her and said, "Don't ever worry about dying. There's nothing to it!" The dream was so vivid that she woke up, astounded. And I believe that he did come to reassure her, because that is precisely the phrase I had heard him use a thousand times to dismiss something as unimportant.

Years before, when news reached me that my mother had died, I was alone in my office, numb with grief. There was a Bible on my desk, and I put my hand on it, staring blindly out the window. As I did so, I felt a pair of hands touch my head, gently, lovingly, unmistakably. Was it an illusion? A hallucination? I don't think so. I think my mother was permitted to reach across the gulf of death to touch and reassure me.

Once when I was preaching at a big church convocation

in Georgia, I had the most startling experience of all. At the end, the presiding bishop asked all the ministers in the audience to come forward and sing a hymn.

Watching them come down the aisles, I suddenly saw my father among them. I saw him as plainly as when he was alive. He seemed about forty, vital and handsome, singing with the others. When he smiled at me and put up his hand in an old familiar gesture, for several unforgettable seconds it was as if my father and I were alone in that big auditorium. Then he was gone. But he was *there,* and I know that someday, somewhere I'll meet him again.

So long, Son . . .

— Arthur Godfrey —

Somewhere in this universe is a timeless, undeniable force. It's stronger than granite, steel, majestic mountains towering into the sky—or nuclear fission.

Sooner or later—in strange and different manifestations—that force touches every human. Sure, some pass it off as a phenomenon that somehow cannot be reduced to an exact scientific formula. To others it is the hand of the Almighty—a reminder that regardless of the grandeur of man and his accomplishments—God is still "running the show" here on earth.

Now, I want to tell you of such an experience. I have remembered it across the years and it will ring in my memory for as long as I live.

It's about my dad—God bless him!

Let me explain a little about my dad. He was one of the most brilliant and warm persons I have ever known. A lecturer, newspaper man, magazine writer, and raconteur—he was at home in any society. He was the well-rounded man I always wanted to be.

Of course, he had his failings, too. One was a disinclination towards business and finance. As a result, he went through several small fortunes and sometimes things were tough at home. That's why I went on my own at fifteen. But I never blamed dad.

All this is prelude to the point I want to make. But, if in telling it—one human, faltering on the precipice of lost faith or shaken belief—takes heart, my telling the story will have been worthwhile.

For out of it, I learned firsthand about that timeless force in this world. Now, whenever the adulation of the crowd dins in my ears . . . whenever temporary wealth and fame assault my senses and balance—it helps me remember that force—transcendent above the world itself.

It makes me remember how the hand of God is at work constantly and I am humble in His presence.

It was in 1923. I was stationed on board a Navy destroyer—in charge of radio communications. I had knocked around a lot since I left home. The years and life had not been too kind but the Navy had been a sanctuary, the only security I had known for a long time. One day, tired, I fell asleep in my bunk and I dreamed.

My dad—I had not seen him for years—suddenly walked into the room. He offered his hand, saying, "So long, son." I answered, "So long, Dad." I said some kind of prayer. It wasn't eloquent, but it came from the heart.

I never saw him again. When I woke up, my buddies told me that at the exact time while I was asleep, the wires from shore hummed the news of my dad's death.

Don't tell me about science and its exact explanation of everything. Some things are bigger. God is the difference. He gets around.

"For Thou Art with Me"

— Faye Field —

On December 9, 1991, I had an unusual dream. I stood alone in a small auditorium. From backstage came a familiar voice: a young man reciting something I couldn't quite make out. Then he said, clearly, "Yea, though I walk through the valley of the shadow of death . . ." I recognized it immediately: the 23rd Psalm! "I will fear no evil: for thou art with me—"

Suddenly the voice stopped and I woke up. It was 2:00 A.M.

I realized the voice in my dream was that of a former student, my sister's son, Samuel C. Washam. The auditorium was in the rural school where I had taught him. He had a good voice and had often stepped out from behind the stage curtains in plays I directed. I had taught him many recitations, but the 23rd Psalm was one of his favorites.

Since then, I had prayed many times for my nephew, who was now middle-aged, terminally ill and lonely. He was afraid, and seemed to have lost his way from God. I had asked the Lord to let Samuel C. know that broken people are dear to his heart. I fell back into a fitful sleep with that same prayer on my lips.

The phone woke me early. It was my sister telling me her son had died. I asked her, "When?"

"Two o'clock this morning," she answered quietly.

I thought of the last words Samuel C. had said in my dream, "For thou art with me." I knew he had found his way again.

The Rose that Wouldn't Die

— Glenn Kittler —

In February 1978, I met a boyhood hero of mine. One of the first movies I can remember seeing was *Hell's Angels,* a picture about fighter pilots in World War I, and it starred Ben Lyon. I remember reading that Ben Lyon did his own flying and even shot some of the combat photography aloft. For a long time, I was Ben Lyon on-the-attack, bent low over my bicycle as I raced around the neighborhood.

Movie stars had a great aura about them in those days. They were our American royalty. For many years, Ben Lyon was the king, before Gable, before Bogart or Spencer Tracy, and he remained a king for me even after he and his lovely wife, Bebe Daniels, moved to England, where they remained stars for another thirty years.

That February, I had the joy and the privilege of spending an afternoon with Ben Lyon at his home in Beverly Hills, where we talked about many things. When we talked about his marriage to Bebe, Ben told me a haunting story. Listening to it, I knew that it was more than a fragment of a great love story. It was also a statement of faith.

Bebe, Ben said, always loved roses. When they were first married and living in California, part of their garden was set aside for what Bebe regarded as her rose chapel. Every morning before leaving for the studio, she would spend several minutes alone among her roses. "Arranging my day," she would explain. But Ben knew these were her moments of prayer and meditation.

In 1933, Bebe and Ben were invited to make some personal appearances in England. They expected to be there just a few months. Instead, they stayed for thirty-eight years. In World War II they chose not to return to the safety of America. They did radio programs for British soldiers overseas, appeared in canteens, toured the combat zones in plays.

When America entered the war in 1941, Ben joined the U.S. Air Force and was assigned to intelligence work. Bebe kept on entertaining the troops. As American servicemen began moving through England, their house in London virtually became a canteen for them. Bebe somehow saw to it that the house was always full of roses. American Beauty roses. Her favorite. After the war they had a television series, made more movies and appeared in more plays. They were busy, happy and very popular with the British people.

Then in 1963, Bebe suffered a stroke that put her in the hospital for several weeks. Eight years later, in 1971, she had another, this a bad one. Doctors told Ben there was not much hope, but this did not stop his prayers. Every morning, he and the children went to Mass and prayed for Bebe. For hours every day they stood at her bedside and prayed. Clergymen of all faiths told them that the whole of England was praying for Bebe.

There seemed to be some improvement, and at last they were able to bring Bebe home, with nurses around the clock. On the evening of March 15, Ben was with Bebe in her room when she awoke from a nap. A phone call came from a close friend of hers, and Ben heard Bebe say: "My dear, I've just been for a walk in the most beautiful rose garden."

She had not, of course. She had been sleeping, perhaps dreaming. By dawn, Bebe was gone.

Thousands of messages of sympathy came from all over the world. A few days later, at the funeral services, the church was a mountain of flowers. There was one wreath from the taxi drivers of London. There was another from the Royal Family.

Ben knew what farewell gesture Bebe would want from him. He had a florist prepare a sheath of forty American Beauty roses—one rose for each year of their marriage. The roses were in the sanctuary during the Mass of the Angels.

The day was cloudy, misty, with a cold wind. As the choir sang "Abide With Me," and reached the words, "Through cloud and sunshine, Lord, abide with me," the sun came out and filled the church with the colors of the stained-glass windows.

All the flowers were sent ahead to the cemetery and were in place when the cortege arrived. They would, Ben knew, be given to children's hospitals later. After the brief service, he impulsively broke off one of the forty roses in the sheath, and took it home. He put the rose in a slender vase, added some water, and placed it on his desk. He did not need the rose to remind him of Bebe. But he felt it was a way to keep her with him a little longer.

Ben expected the rose to live a few days, then fade, so he was pleasantly surprised when the flower was still in bloom after a week. He added fresh water. The rose was still in bloom a month later. Three months later. Six months. One day he noticed that the stem had become petrified, and yet the rose lived on. None of the experts he consulted could explain it.

A year after Bebe died, Ben decided to move back to California. Before leaving London, he took the rose and the slender vase to his son Richard's house, told his daughter-in-law about the rose, and said: "Angela, please do me a favor. Keep this rose in a safe place, on the mantlepiece or somewhere. Just let me know when it dies."

Last September, over seven years after Bebe's death, Ben went back to London to visit his children and grandchildren. In Richard's house, he saw the slender vase on the mantlepiece, the rose still whole on the petrified stem, still perfect.

"I no longer need an explanation for it," Ben told me. "I believe that the rose is God's way of letting us know that Bebe is herself alive, living with Him, waiting for us in that rose garden He showed her as she went to Him. Believing this has made my own faith more meaningful."

Soon after that, our time together ended. It was, I'm sure,

one of the last interviews that Ben Lyon granted. A month later, he died of a heart attack while on a Pacific cruise. For me, his memory will always live on—like that rose.

Happy Mother's Day
— Carolyn Hyden —

It was Mother's Day, and I was especially worried about Mom. This year, for the first time, she would be all alone on the holiday. I kept thinking, *If only Gary were with her.*

My big brother Gary had been a quiet, caring man who loved helping others. Seven years earlier when my father died, Gary moved in with Mom and was a great comfort to her. They loved to play games together, watch TV and read books. Gary took a job at a convenience store close by.

Then one November evening the store was robbed; Gary was shot and killed. Afterward Mom's loneliness was acute, and I never let her out of my prayers.

That Mother's Day I called to see how she was doing. To my surprise she sounded calm, at peace. Then she told me why.

The day before, she had received cards from her five children and seven grandchildren. But walking back from the mailbox, she couldn't help dwelling on the one card she would not be getting, the one child she would never hear from again.

Inside the empty house Mom brewed a cup of tea and reread her cards. Finally she gathered them all together and put them on a bedside shelf for safekeeping. And there on the shelf she spotted a book she'd long intended to read. As she picked it up and turned the pages, out dropped an old faded greeting card with a handwritten message. It read:
"Happy Mother's Day.
Love, Gary."

Yellow-and-White Daisies

— Haven Conner —

I never see a daisy without thinking of Barbara. We were sorority sisters in college. After her engagement, we searched for a silverware pattern—with daisies. As her bridesmaid I carried the same yellow-and-white flowers up the aisle, and daisies were everywhere at the reception.

Barbara and I talked every day. But then a terrible thing happened. I let an argument between our husbands drive a wedge between us. We stopped talking regularly, quit celebrating birthdays together. Suddenly we weren't friends anymore. I kept putting off calling her to make things right, but the regret never left me. Then I learned that Barbara had died, at age thirty-eight.

I agonized over what had been left unsaid. One afternoon I slumped in a chair in my backyard, where we had held Barbara's wedding reception. *O, God*, I prayed, *I'll never forgive myself for not telling Barbara how sorry I am and how much I loved her.*

Tell her now, God seemed to say.

I poured my heart out, just like we used to do. "You were the best friend I ever had," I said. "I'm so sorry." Somehow I felt she had heard me. I got up, trimmed some wayward branches, even mowed the grass. That night I went to bed with a lighter heart. I only wished I had reached out to Barbara when she could still respond.

Next morning, in a corner of the yard, sprouting up from the freshly mowed lawn was an unexpected bouquet—a foot-high clump of yellow-and-white daisies.

The Warning

— George Todd —

The voice woke me from a sound sleep. I was so startled that I sprang out of bed and stood there in the dark, looking around wildly as the words echoed inside my head: "George! George, wake up, wake up! Something's burning!"

Outside, the November night was calm and still in our little town of Oxford on the eastern shore of Maryland. Yet there, in my bedroom, I stood in shock. There was no mistaking that voice; it belonged to my wife, Johanna.

But Johanna had been dead for six years.

Immediately my thoughts flashed back to another night years earlier, just after Johanna and I were married, when she had wakened in the middle of the night crying out those exact words. I had leaped out of bed then too, and I recalled that I seemed to see a white mist—or smoke—eddying around the base of our old brass bed. But Johanna and I had searched the house, and could find nothing wrong. Later we agreed she had simply wakened from a nightmare and triggered my hyperactive imagination.

Now, in my bedroom, just for a moment, that same white mist seemed to be curling around the brass bed. But the bed wasn't there—it had been consigned to storage years ago.

The flashback quickly faded, leaving me puzzled but worried. I hurried downstairs, fearful of what I might find.

Until now I had thought nothing could go wrong in this charming community of small houses, surrounded by woods full of deer and visited each fall by thousands of Canada geese that winter in the area. It's a good place to live, especially for a recovering alcoholic like me. After Johanna died, my drinking had spiraled out of control—until I entered a twelve-step program and turned my problem over to God. I credited Him with my sobriety and figured He had rescued me for a purpose.

As I inspected the downstairs rooms I found nothing amiss. Behind the fire screen in the living room a few dying embers still remained. Nothing alarming. I waited a few minutes, wondering if I had imagined the whole thing.

Then something urged me to go over and place my hand on the wall beside the brick chimney. It was scorching hot! And through a narrow gap between the mantel and the wall I could see flames.

The house was on fire!

Suddenly I felt calm and clearheaded. I picked up the phone, dialed 911 and reported the fire to the dispatcher. Then I heard crackling inside the wall; the fire was spreading upward between the studs, toward the attic. Two houseguests were asleep upstairs.

As I rushed up the steps, the piercing wail of a siren sounded in the distance, summoning Oxford's volunteer fire company. Still I felt that sense of peace. I woke the others, and the three of us calmly walked out just as the fire fighters arrived.

When the fire fighters cut through the roof, a terrifying tongue of flame shot thirty feet into the midnight sky, but thanks to their quick response, the house was saved. The cause of the fire was a defective chimney, and we were lucky to have got out alive.

But a lot more than luck was involved in our escape. I believe that God, who loves us, sent me that warning in a way that would get my attention: I'm usually not aware of dreaming.

When God rescued me from bondage to alcohol, I believed He had a purpose for me. Whatever else He might have for me, I know He wanted me alert, physically and mentally, to receive the warning and deal with the crisis when it came.

And I plan to continue being a careful listener. I want to be just as ready the next time He calls.

A Glimpse of Heaven's Glory

— Janet Fisher —

I don't know why tragedy struck our family that bright October morning. Nor why I, of all people, should have been allowed that glimpse of glory. I only know that a presence greater than human was part of the experience from the beginning.

The strangeness started the evening before, when I allowed six-year-old Travis to play outside past his bedtime. I'd never done this before. Travis's two younger brothers were already asleep in bed, and he should have been too; he had to go to school in the morning, after all. But Tara, the little girl who lived across the street, was playing outdoors late too. Though Tara was a year older, there seemed to be a special bond between her and Travis. I heard their happy shouts as they played hide-and-seek under the enormous stars—just as I used to here in our little mountain town of Challis, Idaho.

And then, later, when I'd called him in at last and he was in his pajamas, he'd suddenly grown so serious. . . .

"Mommy?" Travis had finished his prayers as I sat on the

edge of his bed. He took his hands and placed them tenderly on my cheeks. Such a solemn little face beneath the freckles!

"What, Babe?" I smiled.

"I . . . just love you, Mommy," he said, searching my eyes. "I just want you to know that I love you."

The words remained with me as I got ready for bed. Not that it was unusual for Travis to show affection. His outgoing nature had become even more so after he accepted Jesus as his Savior, at age five. Little children who know Jesus seem to bubble over with love for the whole world. It was the intensity—almost the urgency—with which he'd said the words that was unlike him.

As I lay in bed that night, the sense that something out of the ordinary was about to happen stayed with me. Our house is small, and since my mother came to stay with us I've shared a bedroom with the children. I could hear their soft, restful breaths as they slept. That wasn't what kept me awake. Nor was it the empty space beside me—my husband was now married to another. Yes, our family had certainly had its moments of pain, but our faith had brought us this far.

I thought back to that time, four years before, when I'd realized my need for the Savior and invited Him to take over my struggle. How magnificently He had! So much help had been lavished upon us going through the divorce, the changed life-style, the financial difficulties. From our pastor and church friends I'd gained strength and hope. But it was the conversion of little freckle-faced Travis that brought me the day-by-day lessons.

"Why are you worried, Mommy?" Travis had said so many times, a hint of impatience in his wide brown eyes. "You have Jesus. We'll get the money for that bill." And we always did.

Two in the morning. "I love you, Mommy" still pealed in my ears like some distant, gentle bell. I remembered that as my closeness to Jesus increased, my spirit would sometimes hear messages from Him.

I am preparing Travis for something, I'd heard this silent voice tell me, many times. And this did seem to be the case. Hadn't there been that night a couple of months ago . . . ? I'd awaked before daylight and noticed Travis sitting on his bed . . . just sitting, in the purple predawn.

"What's the matter, Babe?" I had asked him.

"Don't you see them?" He sounded disappointed.

"See what?"

"These two angels."

I breathed in sharply; I saw only the familiar room. The boy was wide awake, perfectly calm. I asked him if he was afraid.

"No, Mommy," he'd said. I waited by his bed a little while. Then he said, "Okay, they're gone, you can go to bed now." That was all. But thinking back on that experience, I felt again that sense of the extraordinary pressing close upon us.

The morning of October 28 dawned bright and still. There was the usual bustle of getting breakfast, finding socks that matched, pencils with erasers and so on. Ten minutes before the time he usually left to walk to school Travis became suddenly agitated:

"Mommy, I've got to go now."

"Babe, it's early. You've got lots of time. Sit down."

"I've got to go now! I've just got to!" Travis cried.

"Why?" I asked in bewilderment. He mumbled something about his teacher, about not being late. It didn't make sense: He was never late. "Wait a few minutes," I insisted. "Finish your cocoa."

"Mommy, please!" To my amazement big tears were rolling down his cheeks.

"All right, all right, go ahead," I told him, shaking my head at the commotion. He dashed out the door, a hurrying little figure pulling on a tan jacket. Across the street, little Tara was coming down her walk. I saw the two children meet and set off toward Main Street together.

Five minutes later I was clearing away the breakfast dishes when it happened. A shudder of the floor beneath me, then a hideous screech of writhing wood. There had never been an earthquake in Challis, but I knew we were having an earthquake now. I ran from the house calling over my shoulder, "I've got to get to Travis!"

I was at the driveway when another tremor flung me against the car. I waited till the earth stopped heaving, then climbed into the driver's seat.

I'd gone two blocks when I saw a woman standing beside a pile of rubble on the sidewalk, the debris of a collapsed storefront. The look on her face was one of nightmare horror.

Unrolling the window, I was surprised at the calmness of my voice as I asked, "Was someone . . . caught?"

"Two children," the white face said thinly. "One in a tan jacket . . ."

I drove swiftly on. Past people running toward the damaged building. Around the corner. To the school. Oh, I knew. I knew already. But maybe (please God!), maybe farther down the street there'd be two children standing bewildered at a curbside. There were not, of course. I drove back to the rubble heap.

Then a numb blur of events: police, firemen, people struggling with the debris. Identification. Arms around me. I was at the clinic. I was being driven home. I was in my living room again. My mother was there, and I was telling her and my two little boys what had happened. Mother was praying.

Suddenly, as I sat there in the living room, perhaps even in mid-sentence—I don't know how long it took—I was being lifted right out of the room, lifted above it all, high into the sky, and placed by a beautiful gate. A cluster of happy people stood within the gate. In utter amazement I began recognizing the youthful, robust faces: Dad, my favorite aunt, Grandpa . . . and in the center of them all, the radiant form of Jesus! As I watched, He stretched out His hands to welcome a child who was approaching, a smiling boy dressed in what seemed to be an unbleached muslin tunic over long trousers of the same homespun-looking fabric. Travis ran forward and grasped the hand of Jesus, looking up at Him with eager brown eyes. The cluster of people welcomed my son, and he seemed to recognize them, although some he had never met. As the joyful group turned to leave, Travis suddenly turned his shining face toward me.

"It's really neat here, Mommy."

"I know, Babe." My throat felt choked, and I don't know whether I spoke aloud or not.

"I really like it here."

"I know."

"Mommy . . . I don't want to go back."

"It's okay, Babe." And it was okay, in that transcendent moment. Nothing I could ever do, nothing that could ever happen here on earth, could make Travis as happy as I saw him right then. When I looked around me, I was back in my home.

That's where the long battle of grief was fought, of course: in the kitchen with its empty chair, in the bedroom where he'd said his good-night prayers, and the yard where he'd played hide-and-seek. Transcendent moments do not last— not for us on earth. Three years have passed since the day of the earthquake, passed among the daily routines of cleaning, cooking, chauffeuring, praying.

But neither do such moments fade. That scene at heaven's threshold is as vivid in each detail today as in the measureless instant when I was allowed to see. I have been granted another glimpse since then, this time of Tara among a group of joyfully playing children, all dressed in those tuniclike garments. (I did not see Travis this time, nor anyone else I recognized.)

Tara's mother understands no better than I the why of a

child's death, the why of heaven's glory. I know only that both are real, and that—when we hear the answer at last—it will start with the words, "I love you."

A Father's Care

— Stephen G. Gladish —

In 1992 my sister Joy was fighting her final battle against cancer. I wanted Joy to go into a hospice here in Tucson, where we both lived, but she didn't want to leave her home. I couldn't be with her constantly. *God, who will watch over her?*

Joy and I had come from a medical family. Mom was a nurse. Dad was a small-town GP in Glenview, Illinois, twenty miles north of Chicago. His concern for his patients was legendary; he often made house calls without being summoned. Sometimes Joy and I had felt overlooked, longing for the attention he seemed to reserve for his patients. But no matter how busy he'd been all week, Dad stood on the basement stairs every Sunday morning, polishing his shoes for church.

I called Dr. Marilyn Croghan, Joy's radiologist, hoping she could convince Joy to move into a hospice. "Your father called also," she said. "He wants Joy to come live with him when we've done all we can medically . . ." Her beeper went off, and the doctor was abruptly called away before I could correct her.

Three days later Joy died at home. I called Dr. Croghan to thank her for all she'd done. Then I mentioned the phone call. "It had to be someone else," I said.

"He *distinctly* said he was Joy's father," Dr. Croghan insisted. "He talked about her case and understood all the medical details—as if he were a doctor too."

And then I knew God had provided the reassurance I needed. Dad died in 1967, but he still watched over his children.

GOD'S PLAN
INCLUDES US

Let your work be manifest to your servants . . . and prosper for us the work of our hands. . . .
—Psalm 90:16–17 (NRSV)

We give thanks to God always for you all . . . remembering without ceasing your work of faith, and labor of love, and patience of hope in our Lord Jesus Christ. . . .
—I Thessalonians 1:2–3

Our Part of the Circle

— Joyce Reagin —

December 7, 1980, was one of those pre-Christmas Sundays that was meant to be full of candles, carols and great expectations. After church my husband, Earl, and I planned to take our young sons for a holiday portrait. Then a ride to look at neighborhood Christmas decorations would put us in the mood for a family shopping trip punctuated by whisperings and giggled secrets.

We missed church. On top of that, Grant, age seven, and his brother, Britt, age four, did *not* want to get dressed up for a photograph sitting. They whined all the way to the studio, where the photographer could find no evidence of our appointment and could not work us in. The ensuing Christmas ride was more dismal yet. But the capper was yet to come. We reached home only to discover that the rest of our Christmas money was gone. I had lost about a hundred dollars in cash.

A hundred dollars might not be a lot of money to lose, but it was important to us because we had, for the first time in our marriage, managed to adhere strictly to a Christmas budget.

Perhaps I'd been a little too proud! That very afternoon, while riding around in the car, I'd drawn the gray bank envelope from my purse and shown the bills inside to Earl and the boys. "Aren't you proud of me? Mom's actually managed to budget the Christmas money!"

That was the last time any of us saw the envelope. Evidently I had not put it back into my purse but had laid it on the seat. During the course of our afternoon stops, it must have fallen unnoticed from the car.

"It's Christmas," I explained to Earl. "People *steal* money this time of year. I'm sure someone has found it. An envelope full of cash, with no name, no identification! Who could blame someone for keeping it?"

All evening I stewed. As we prepared for bed, Earl put his arms around me and kissed me. "Please, darling, stop thinking about the money. Tomorrow we'll retrace our steps. Who knows? Maybe someone has turned it in." We prayed together that I'd have peace about the money and that we'd find it again if it was God's will.

It didn't help a bit. I tossed and turned all night.

The next morning it was difficult to concentrate on teaching my classes at school. I kept thinking about the lost money, about my carelessness, my stupidity, about the gifts we still had to buy.

And then it came to me—the $200.

Since early fall, Earl and I had set aside $200 in a savings account because we felt God wanted us to give that money to an individual or family in need. We'd been asking God to direct our path.

Then a stronger, inner voice reminded me, that was not our money, that was God's money. As tempting as it was, that money was not for me to spend.

After work, Earl and I retraced our path. No one had turned in money at the filling station where we'd bought gas. Nor had anything been found at the cemetery, where we'd taken flowers to my grandmother's grave. The driveway at our own home was empty, of course.

But a change was beginning to take place in me. At home that night, I went into the bedroom and knelt alone. "Dear God," I prayed, "I can't stand this worried feeling. Please help me to release this matter to you. I know that *all* of our money is Yours, including that hundred dollars. If it's Your will, please return the money to us. If it's not, I release that money, I give it freely to You and, through You, to whoever found it.

"And," I added, "I also release my carelessness on Sunday. If You can use even that for good, please go ahead. In Jesus' name, amen."

A peace stole over me. Not surprisingly, the house seemed brighter. The boys started laughing again, and we all joined in on snatches of carols.

The next day the sky was the brilliant blue that God saves for winter skies. I hummed as I headed for school, and taught my lessons without even thinking of the money.

Then, just before break time, I heard a still, small voice. *Go and call the places where you stopped on Sunday.*

But God, I thought, *we went back to all those places yesterday.*

Go and call.

Obediently, excitedly, I hurried to the phone. First I called the gas station. "I may have lost some money there," I began.

"No," the lady clipped.

Next was the cemetery. I felt funny about making that call, but I dialed anyway. The manager answered.

Feeling foolish, I said, "Last Sunday I lost some money—"

He interrupted me. "How much?"

"Almost a hundred dollars. The money was stuffed into a gray bank envelope."

"How about ninety-six dollars?" he asked.

"You have it!" I exclaimed.

"Sure do. A gravedigger found it while he was picking up trash. He turned it in, said he thought it might be somebody's Christmas money."

After school I rushed to the cemetery office. The man who found it, Rubin Sales, was not there. Holding the dirt-smeared, tire-streaked envelope, I marveled that he had even bothered to look inside.

"Please tell him thank you," I said, leaving $10 for him.

I wasn't even out of the cemetery before that quiet voice spoke once more. *Rubin Sales is the one I want you to give the two hundred dollars to.* Excitedly I went to find Earl.

The very next day we went back to the cemetery to meet

Rubin Sales. He was a middle-aged man, tall and muscular. But when we introduced ourselves, he looked at us almost shyly.

"Mr. Sales," I said, "thank you so much for finding and returning our money. Now we'd like to give some to you."

He firmly shook his head no without speaking.

"But, Mr. Sales—" I started.

"Thank you," he said, "but no. No reward. When I first saw that envelope, it just looked like trash. But something told me to look inside. Then something told me that was somebody's Christmas money." He paused. "I grew up poor. I know what it's like to hope and pray for something. And I didn't want any children's hopes not to come true."

"You don't understand," Earl answered. "This isn't a reward This is God's money. We've been keeping it until He told us what to do with it. And we believe He's told us this two hundred dollars is yours."

No one spoke for a moment. Earl's odd pronouncement hung in the chilly air.

"*Exactly* two hundred dollars?" Sales asked. His voice had a strange crack to it.

We nodded.

"I've been scrimping and saving to meet my bills," he said, "and last night when I sat down to pay them, there wasn't even near enough. As I worried what to do, a program about world hunger came on the television. When I saw the faces of those starving children, my own problems seemed so tiny. I wanted to help so badly, but all I could do was pray. I prayed for a way to pay my bills so I could send the money I *had* saved to help those little ones."

"And how much are your bills?" Earl asked, although we already knew the answer.

"Exactly two hundred dollars," he said.

"Merry Christmas, Mr. Sales," I said as we handed him the envelope.

He Sent Me

— Roberta L. Messner —

One summer day a friend told me of visiting a hospital and praying with a terminally ill woman. She'd learned that the woman was distressed about what would happen to her husband and her preschool son after her death. The story touched me, and over the next few months I found myself praying about this sad situation. I asked God to send someone especially to help that poor motherless boy.

Shortly before Christmas my husband's truck was in need of repair; he took it to a mechanic who'd been recommended to him and who lived far out in the country. When he came home, my husband said, "That mechanic's having a tough time making ends meet." Apparently the man was a widower with a young boy to bring up, and he was really up against it. Then my husband came up with an idea: "What do you think of our taking that little kid Christmas shopping?"

I quickly agreed, and with the father's permission, that's just what we did. We drove out, picked up the youngster and gave him a day filled with all kinds of holiday fun—and some presents to boot.

Of course, you know the end of this story. The mechanic was the husband, and the boy was the son, of the woman I'd been praying for. And what about the "someone" I'd asked God to send to help? Well, He'd sent *me*.

State Fair

— Janet Morris Yearwood —

A trip to the State Fair was an annual expedition for us. Every year we went—for the rides, the exhibits, the food, but most of all to do something together as a family. This year was no different. Packed into the station wagon, the children were bursting with excitement. Only Mike and I were glum. This was a last family outing before we broke the news to the children that soon we wouldn't be living together. We were headed for divorce.

As I looked across at Mike in the driver's seat, I wondered how things could have got this bad. We'd met twenty years earlier, when we were both teachers at the same school. A math instructor, Mike was the strong, silent type. An English major, I was prone to talk about anything and everything. After a few dates we fell hard for each other and in ten months we were married.

Over the years the children came, first Tom, then Katherine, then Caroline. Financial pressures quickly followed. Mike quit teaching to work in computers, and I became a stay-at-home mother. Even though we lived a very modest life-style, money was always tight. Communication between us became increasingly strained, and whenever we argued it was always about money.

Now everything seemed to be falling apart. We'd just bought a bigger house, and I had gone back to work full-time as an editorial assistant to help pay our bills. That meant putting three-year-old Caroline into day care, which made me feel like a failure as a mother. And the job hunt had been tough on my self-esteem. At the same time, Mike and I grew more distant.

We went to a marriage enrichment weekend at our church, but the solutions were short-lived. I had several counseling sessions with our pastor, but communication with Mike didn't improve. Night after night I prayed for our marriage, but the rift between us only grew. Separation and divorce seemed the only answer.

At the State Fair the two of us watched silently as the children scampered from ride to ride. Then we wandered aimlessly through the booth-filled exhibition hall. Vendors called to us, but we were lost in our thoughts and paid little attention to them—until a short, balding salesman in a sport shirt and a baseball cap came up to me. "Young lady, would you like to register for our drawing?" He was a representative for *Encyclopaedia Britannica,* and he wondered if besides entering the drawing we wanted to look at a set.

For some reason I stopped to listen to him. Maybe it was his warm smile. Maybe it was his friendly tone of voice. Maybe it was because as a former English teacher I could never resist looking at a book. "Sure," I said.

Mike and I followed him to his booth and sat down, content to rest our weary feet for a moment. Katherine and Caroline, who were still with us, were shown to a nearby picnic table, where the man had an assortment of crayons and coloring books.

As we filled out our names, the salesman started to extol the virtues of the encyclopedia. He talked about its breadth of knowledge, the range of subjects included. He showed us how to look up different topics, like great white sharks or the names of baseball players, his hands running over the gold letters on the spine as he drew out each volume. "Or if you wanted to teach your children more about Jesus Christ," he said, "you'd go right to the extensive listings about Christianity."

Before we knew what was happening, he asked if we wanted to order the set of books. Mike and I looked helplessly at each other, knowing full well we wouldn't be living together in a few weeks, knowing full well that a set of encyclopedias wasn't something we could split up. To my astonishment Mike said yes.

While the salesman started filling in forms, Mike and I sat speechless. What in the world were we doing? Why were we making an investment like this when we'd soon have two separate households to support? Why were we acting as though we were a happily married couple?

"What would you like written on the presentation page?"

the salesman asked. "We can print something like 'From Mom and Dad to the kids.' " He looked over at Katherine and Caroline quietly drawing pictures at the picnic table. "You've got such a nice family. I'm sure you want to say something for the children."

Suddenly hot tears burned my eyes and I turned my head to hide them. Soon there'd be no more "Mom and Dad." We wouldn't be together to pore over the pages of these books, helping the kids with their homework, looking up items for a term paper or essay. What sort of gift could it be without our involvement?

I remembered the encyclopedia we'd had when I was a girl and how Mom and Dad guided me through it. Dad was a Baptist minister, and I remember us looking at maps of the Holy Land, Dad's finger tracing Moses' route from Egypt to Canaan. It wouldn't have meant anything without his help.

I think the presentation page should read, 'From Mama and Papa to Tom, Katherine and Caroline.' " Mike said. "Don't you, Janet?"

"Yes," I said, "I think so."

The salesman returned to his writing and I looked over at Mike. Maybe he still thought of us as an inseparable team. Maybe we could change our minds. Maybe we could still work things out.

"I don't think we've ever made a decision so quickly," I said to the salesman as I stood to shake his hand. "You're certainly good at your job."

And then he said an unusual thing, something that seemed

odd for a salesman who was closing a transaction. "Let's give the credit to God," he replied quietly. "He gave me whatever ability I have."

We left the booth and returned to the busy aisle. As the children ran ahead, I looked up hesitantly into Mike's eyes. He looked down at me and grinned. Putting his arm around my shoulder, he gave me a squeeze and said, "Peace offering."

It was nothing more than that, but in that split second, we both knew we should try again. More than that, this time I knew we'd make it. A total stranger had given us new hope. Suddenly I wanted to go back and thank him.

We found the salesman back at the *Encyclopaedia Britannica* booth rearranging his books, getting ready for another customer and presentation. "May we talk with you a minute?" I asked.

His warm smile returned. I stammered, "I—I just wanted to tell you that when we came here today, my husband and I were contemplating divorce. We didn't think we could go on anymore. But there was something in the way you talked about our family and God that made us think again . . ." I paused, unable to finish.

"Can you step outside?" the salesman asked. "There's something I have to say."

We made our way out of the stuffy, crowded building and into the fresh air. The noise of the State Fair was still going on around us, but for a moment we three felt we were all alone.

"I just returned from a business trip to California," he said. "And I've had a lot of problems of my own at home. I wasn't sure I wanted to come to work today. Now I know why I did. God sent your family to me. You're the reason I was supposed to be here today."

That was the last time we saw the salesman, but we have the result of his sale on our shelves. I treasure it. It reminds me of how much we almost lost, and how much we gained. Not just twenty-nine volumes from "a capella" to "zygote," but an inner knowledge of how precious a marriage is and how important it is to work at preserving it. "From Mama and Papa," the presentation page says. We'll do everything we can to keep those names together.

Slow Boat to China

— Lucy Noordhoof —

In 1959 my husband and I were dismayed when our mission board announced it was sending us to Taiwan by freighter, a long voyage that would seem even longer with our two children: Nancy, three, and Sammy, still in diapers.

Surely it would be easier to fly, we said. But we were told that the board had to send another couple with children, the Howards, to the Philippines via the freighter. Since children were not allowed as passengers without a doctor onboard, we were to go because my husband, Sam, is a plastic surgeon.

From the time we boarded in Los Angeles we had our hands full. One parent had to be with the children at all times for fear they'd fall down a ladder or into the Pacific. Then Sammy got the mumps, and one by one so did the other youngsters. On the twenty-third day we said good-bye to the Howards, and two days later, exhausted, we landed in Taiwan.

The years hurried by. Sammy returned to the United States for college. At school he was often homesick, wishing he had someone to talk to about life in Asia. Then one day in the library a tall girl came up to him. "You may not remember me," she began, "but I'm Vicky Howard. About seventeen years ago you gave me the mumps."

Three years later Vicky and Sammy were married. They moved back to Taiwan and now we have grandchildren right on our alley. Today whenever I recall that long, tedious voyage, I can see how God's plan was unfolding, even on a slow boat to China.

"I'll Share My Son with You"

— Evelyn Myer Allison —

As young Navy wives in Norfolk, Virginia, my neighbor Darleen and I developed a close bond. We even shared the same due date for our second babies. We each already had a daughter, so we were both thinking "blue."

Then, four months into my pregnancy, I miscarried. Darleen consoled me, but I still felt a pang of jealousy when she gave birth to a beautiful boy. As my two-year-old daughter, Cyndi, sat in a rocking chair cuddling baby Jimmy, I broke down. *God*, I prayed, *please let me be happy for Darleen*.

Darleen put her arm around me. "I'll always share my son with you," she promised.

Just as Jimmy was taking his first wobbly steps, Darleen moved to Kansas. We kept in touch, but it took us fifteen years to arrange a trip to visit. I couldn't believe my eyes when I saw handsome, almost-grown Jimmy.

Shortly after, we moved to North Carolina, where we got word that Jimmy had joined the Navy and was stationed nearby. On his first leave, he didn't have enough time to make it back home to Kansas, so he came to stay with us. "He always has a home here," I wrote to Darleen.

Jimmy started coming to visit quite a bit. He palled around with Cyndi, and they became fast friends. But then I noticed something more: Cyndi and Jimmy were in love.

On their wedding day, I remembered Darleen's promise to me all those years before: "I'll always share my son with you." Today we also share two grandsons.

The Sign of the Dolphin

— Sue Monk Kidd —

When my close friend Betty was hospitalized with cancer, she called me one morning to say she'd had a vivid dream. She was drowning in a vast body of water when a dolphin swam toward her and pulled her to shore. It was the first real hope I'd heard in her voice.

Feeling a sudden inspiration, I called all over town searching for a helium-filled dolphin balloon to tie on her bed. Believe it or not, I found one. Throughout her hospitalization it floated over her bed, a smiling sign of hope. "I pray one day God sends you a dolphin when you need one," she said, hugging me.

A year went by and Betty recovered, despite an uncertain prognosis. That summer I walked along a lonely stretch of beach on Harbor Island, South Carolina, unable to shake a mild feeling of depression. Numerous problems awaited me back home and they seemed to be looming larger and larger in my mind. I waded into the ocean and stood where the sand dropped off sharply and curved into Helena Sound. Suddenly

I was startled by a smiling bottle-nose dolphin, which splashed out of the water twenty yards away. He dived and surfaced before me in a shining, spinning spray of joy. I began to laugh, feeling an exhilarating wonder. And somehow in those moments, my problems found their way back into perspective and the depression dissolved.

I can't help but wonder if God answered Betty's prayer and sent me that dolphin. It's so like Him, isn't it, to send us help when we need it? To send balloons and dolphins and friends to meet the needs His children feel.

God's Wonders
Work for Us

For you are great and do wondrous things; you alone are God.
—Psalm 86:10 (NRSV)

"Jesus of Nazareth, a man attested to you by God with deeds of power, wonders, and signs. . . ."
—Acts 2:22 (NRSV)

The Search

— John Gleason —

It happened years ago, but the incident sticks in mind and memory. Perhaps I can make you see why.

It was October, 1938. I had just graduated from Northwestern University and wanted to see something of the world before settling into a career. With $350 saved from a summer job—quite a lot in those days—I was heading for Puerto Rico and the Virgin Islands, places that seemed romantic to me.

In New York I boarded a rusty old coal-burning freighter. At first there seemed to be just three passengers besides myself: a bright young civil engineer from Michigan, a worried-looking old man in a white linen suit and a stately, charming woman who turned out to be Mrs. Charles Colmore, wife of the Episcopal Bishop of Puerto Rico, who was returning there after a visit to relatives in the United States.

We made friends quickly, the way you do on a sea voyage. Then, two days out of New York, a young woman with dull blond hair appeared on deck for the first time. She was in her early twenties, much too thin. She looked so pale and wan that we instantly pitied her. She seemed a bit wary of us male passengers, but she accepted Mrs. Colmore's invitation for tea in her cabin.

"It's a strange story," the bishop's wife told us later. "She comes from a little town in Pennsylvania and she's on her way to the West Indies to look for her husband. He evidently left home several months ago after a violent quarrel with the girl's mother over his drinking and his inability to find a job and support his wife properly. The girl finally heard a rumor that her husband had gone to the West Indies. She still loves him, so she left her old dragon of a mother, and now she's on her way to find Billy—that's her husband's name: Billy Simpson."

"You mean," I said incredulously, "she's going to leave the ship when we get to San Juan and start looking? Why, that's crazy! There are hundreds of islands in the Caribbean; maybe thousands."

"I told her that," the bishop's wife said, "but it didn't seem to make any impression. She just says she'll find him. How, I don't know. But she seems absolutely sure of it."

"It would take a miracle," the old man said, thin and intense in his white tropic suit and brown wool cap.

"It would take a whole hatful of miracles," I muttered.

"Does she have any friends where she's going?" asked the young engineer. "Does she have any money?"

"No friends," said the bishop's wife. "And almost no money. Ten dollars, I think she said. Not even enough to get her back to New York."

When we heard this, the rest of us dug into our pockets

and raised twenty-five dollars to give to this strange waif of a girl.

"This will help you find a place to stay when we get to San Juan," the bishop's wife said when she presented the money in front of all of us. "And I'm sure our church there will help find enough for your return passage home."

The girl murmured her thanks. Then she said, "But I'm not going home. I'm going to find my husband."

"Where? How?" asked the old man. He had been fired from his bookkeeping job after thirty years with the same company. Now he was moving to Puerto Rico, where he hoped his experience would outweigh his age when it came to finding a job. I couldn't help thinking that he was seeking an answer to his own where and how as much as to the girl's.

The girl shrugged and smiled a little. She had the oddest smile—sad, fateful, dreamlike. "Prayers," she said. "My prayers. A few years ago, I asked God to send me someone to love, and He did, and I married him. Now I'm asking God to help me find my husband again. That's all. Just asking. And I'm sure He will."

The engineer turned away. "Not rational," he murmured, and I nodded. He was a tall, friendly fellow on his way to become a plantation overseer on Santo Domingo. He was a couple of years older than I, and it made me feel like a man of the world to agree with him. The old man said nothing. The bishop's wife looked thoughtful. We didn't discuss the matter again.

Time passed, trancelike, the way it does on shipboard, the

girl leaning against the rail watching the flying fish skitter across the cobalt sea, the engineer and I on the fantail listening interminably to his record of "Once in Awhile," the old man asking the bishop's wife for ideas about getting a job in Puerto Rico.

We docked in San Juan early one morning. I was scheduled to catch another boat that afternoon for St. Thomas in the Virgin Islands, and so had a few hours to kill. The others were going to look for an inexpensive hotel where the girl could stay while she figured out her next move, whatever that might be. The engineer and the old man needed a place to stay, too. The bishop's wife had delayed her own trip to Ponce, where the bishop was, in order to give some reassurance to the girl. "I've got to see her settled somewhere," she said to me privately. "And then I'll ask some people at the church to keep an eye on her. She has this unshakable faith, and I've done some praying myself, but . . ."

"But she needs that hatful of miracles, doesn't she?" I said.

Mrs. Colmore smiled. "A great big hat," she said. "A God-sized one, perhaps."

In the smothering heat of midday we walked all over the old city of San Juan, finding the cheap hotels—all run-down establishments infested with fleas and bedbugs. Finally the bishop's wife suggested that we get on a bus for the little neighboring town of San Terce. She thought accommodations might be more attractive and more available there.

So we clambered onto a bus for San Terce, but all the hotels we found in this pleasanter suburb were too expensive.

Finally, exhausted under the hot sun, the bishop's wife, the old man and the girl sat down on a sidewalk bench. The young engineer and I continued the search and, amazingly, we found a pleasant, clean and inexpensive hotel within a block.

We tried to register for the group, but the clerk insisted in broken English that each person register individually. So I went and brought the others into the lobby, where they lined up before the registration book. When it was the girl's turn to sign, she picked up the pen, glanced at the page, dropped the pen—and fainted.

The clerk dashed for some water. The engineer and I put the girl on a couch, and the bishop's wife bathed her forehead while the old man patted her hand. After some water, she came to slowly.

"Heat too much for you?" I asked sympathetically.

She shook her head. "No . . . Billy."

"Billy?"

"He's in the book," the girl whispered.

We jumped up to take a look. There, scrawled after a date two days before, we read: "Billy Simpson."

"Billy Simpson! What room is he in?" I asked the clerk. I couldn't believe it.

"Simpson?" the clerk said. "Oh, he got a job. He come back after work. Not here now."

"This can't be," the old man said almost angrily when the clerk's description of Billy Simpson seemed to fit the girl's. "She must have had some idea that he was here!"

Still lying on the couch, the girl didn't hear, but the

bishop's wife looked at us. "No, I'm sure she didn't," she said. "Otherwise she would have come directly to this hotel on her own, wouldn't she?"

Nobody could answer that. It was obvious that there could be no final answer until Billy Simpson came back from work—by which time I was supposed to be on the boat that sailed overnight to the Virgin Islands.

Now, I know that in a good story the narrator does not remove himself from the scene just when the climactic episode is coming up. But this is the way it all happened. I guess real life doesn't always write the script the way a good playwright would.

Anyway, I had to go. The engineer shook my hand and wished me well. The bishop's wife gave me a letter of introduction to the Episcopal minister on St. Thomas, a Reverend Edwards. The old man said he would come and see me off.

The boat for St. Thomas was belching smoke, more of a ferry than a ship. As we neared the gangway, the old man spoke. "The real reason I wanted to come along was to ask you something. Do you think that prayer really led that girl to her husband?"

"I don't know," I replied uneasily. "There's always coincidence. But this is certainly a big coincidence."

He took my arm. "I wonder if prayer could help me?" he said. "I just wanted to ask you. I don't know much about it."

"Neither do I," I said. "Why don't you ask the bishop's wife? She prayed for the girl, you know."

"Do you think I should? I've been a bit afraid to."

"Sure," I said. "Ask her. And if I hear of any jobs in the Virgin Islands, I'll write you at the hotel."

"Thanks," he said. "Have a good trip." He waved to me from the dock after I was aboard.

When I arrived, Reverend Edwards invited me to stay with him, charging only ten dollars a week for room and board. Settled in, I spent my time sight-seeing, chatting with natives at the docks, writing, relaxing, learning all I could about the islands. Evenings I often visited with Reverend Edwards after dinner. One night I told him about the girl on the boat and the missing husband and the prayers, and probably my tone clearly indicated my doubts about it all.

The old clergyman said: "Don't ever be afraid to believe, John. You're too young to have a closed mind."

With time, the girl and Billy Simpson almost slipped from memory. But one day I mentioned the incident to two new friends of mine, deaconesses who lived next door to the church.

"Why," said one of them, "that Mr. Simpson sounds like a Mr. Simpson we had here at the church clinic. He came from Antigua with a very bad case of the D.T.'s. We practically had to chain him to a bed."

"And then," said the other, "one day he suddenly became alert and insisted on getting up. Our Danish doctor said he'd better stay with us for a time, but Mr. Simpson was adamant. He said he had to get to San Juan to see someone. When we asked who, he said he didn't know. He just had to get to San Juan. That night he caught a small power boat going to Puerto

Rico. We gave him twenty dollars to get him there and maybe enough for a room. That's the last we heard of him. Now this!"

We compared dates, and this "Mr. Simpson" would have landed in Puerto Rico three days before my group arrived in San Juan from New York. He could have reached that hotel two days before we had, as the register showed.

I had to find out. I wrote to the bishop's wife, gave her my news and asked for hers. In two weeks, her answer came: "Yes, it was the right Billy Simpson. His reunion with his wife was one of the most touching things I've ever seen. Now, there have to be several events to consider, miracles possibly. One, Mr. Simpson's sudden cure from alcoholism in St. Thomas, which he confirms; two, his strange compulsion to get to San Juan, which he couldn't understand himself at the time; three, the guidance that led him to that particular hotel; four, his finding a good job within twenty-four hours, after not being able to get a job for months; five, the guidance that took our group to that hotel, a hotel which you yourself found. For me, these events add up to a hatful of miracles that can be explained in only one word: *prayer*. The Simpsons are living happily in San Juan now. Not long ago they gave me fifty dollars to use for charity, and so I am enclosing twenty dollars for your friends who helped Mr. Simpson while he was ill."

I sat with Mrs. Colmore's letter in my lap for a long time.

A week later, I received a letter from the old man. He had gone to Ponce with the bishop's wife, found a good job, joined the church and become very happy in it. He wrote: "When we were all at the hotel that day, Mrs. Colmore said that maybe there was a lesson in the experience we had just shared. I believe there was. For me, the lesson was that some people instinctively know the power of prayer, but others have to learn it."

I couldn't argue with that.

These days, forty years later, my mind is no longer so young, it is no longer closed, and I am no longer afraid to believe.

God's Timing

— Karen Pane —

Everything started out wrong that winter morning. My brother, Bruce, had an errand to do and was late meeting me for our drive to work. When I stepped outside to wait for him, I shivered in the cold. I dashed back into the house, threw off my jacket and grabbed my full-length leather coat. By the time Bruce and I left, we were snarled in rush-hour traffic.

I turned off the expressway only to be blocked by a sanitation truck. I threw the car into reverse. Just then we heard screams: "Help, help! My baby!"

Smoke and flames were gushing out of a fourth-floor window where a woman clutched a baby in her arms. We scrambled out of the car. Bruce ran to a fire alarm box, then raced back. "Quick," he said to me, "your coat." In an instant I took off my long leather coat and we held it between us. "Drop the baby," Bruce yelled.

The baby seemed to float gently down to us, landing right in the center of my coat. She was dressed in a pink snowsuit with her hands tucked in. She gazed up at me, then closed her eyes and fell asleep.

Soon the firemen arrived and rescued the mother. As she was rushed to the ambulance, she called out, "Where's my baby?"

"The baby's fine," I assured her.

I was very late arriving at work. Then I thought back to what had happened that morning. Bruce's errand, my change of coat, the snarled traffic, the sanitation truck . . . Yes, our timing was off that day, but God's timing was perfect.

Appointment in Escambia Bay

— Glenn McDonald —

From the start I had a peculiar feeling about the trip.

"It's an emergency," the caller had said. Down at Escambia Bay, a railroad bridge was damaged; its swing-trestle wouldn't open. They wanted a repair crew from the company I owned, and they wanted it there by six the next morning.

I remember sitting alone in the office after I put the phone down. It was after working hours and all my men had gone home. If I accepted the job, I'd need a barge with a crane and the only one available was twenty-seven miles away at Chico Bayou. That would mean driving there immediately; what's more, I'd have to spend the night on the water tugging the rig back. *Doggone it,* I thought, *I'm not going to do it.*

Yet now, here I was, somewhere in Escambia Bay off the Pensacola coastline. *Little Mac,* my tough thirty-foot work-boat, was chugging away with all its diesel cylinders, its nose locked into the barge ahead with steel cables. It was hard, slow going. The barge was seventy feet long and thirty feet wide.

The crane itself weighed forty tons; it rose above us fifty feet in the air.

I flashed a light at my watch. Eight o'clock. I shook my head and nervously chewed my lip. I didn't like the spot we were in. It was dark, we were off course, and a fog was thickening around us.

The fog. Another reason for not making this trip. During the past weeks the fog had been giving us a lot of trouble, unusually thick stuff, settling in early at night. It would have been wiser to wait until daytime to get the barge, when the sun had burned the fog away. But no, I'd picked up the phone and called Bill Kenney, who lived closer to the office than any of my other men. He was young, strong, and like me, a salvage man and a diver.

Bill's willingness to work a double shift had seemed to settle it: I would make the night trip to bring the barge back.

But *still* I'd hesitated. I put in a call to Janet, and our home phone just rang and rang. Janet, our three girls and I are exceptionally close. I never like the idea of being away from them at night, especially *all* night.

Yet here I was out on *Little Mac*, doing the very thing that common sense said I shouldn't be doing. I worried about whether Janet had received the message from the friend I'd phoned.

Nine o'clock.

The fog swirled around us like clammy gray velvet. We were running on compass; no use trying to spot the channel markers. I reduced the speed to two knots. "Better go up to the bow and keep a lookout," I shouted to Bill over the noise of the engine. "Somebody might be anchored in this muck." We were running slow enough to avoid a collision, but I was uneasy.

Zoom! An airplane. The scream of jet engines reverberated around us in the thick air. We couldn't see the plane, but it seemed to be flying close to us, too close.

Zoom! There was another one. Obviously we must be near one of the Pensacola airport approaches. I looked up at the crane that disappeared into the fog above us, and the thought ran through my head, *What if one of those planes clipped that boom?* All of a sudden I began to have an eerie feeling, the odd sensation of being some kind of target, a helpless tool in a plot I didn't understand, a passenger on a voyage I hadn't wanted to take to a place I didn't want to be. I tried to shrug it off. What was it all about, anyway?

Suddenly, out of the sky behind us, with a high-pitched whine, came another plane. I could see it. Its lights blurred through the fog, a 727 jet, and it was angling down. "He's going to hit!" I screamed. Bill rushed up to me and the two of us watched helplessly as the huge plane plunged through the fog and slammed into the bay. There was a terrible sound of rending metal. Fountains of water exploded into the sky as the lights on the jet went out. Then eerie silence.

Holding my breath, I waited for an explosion; none came. I could see that the plane hadn't disintegrated; the fuselage remained intact. Quickly I ran to our spotlight and started playing it on the 727's cabin. It was settling lower as water poured in, but no one seemed to be coming out. Were they all dead?

Bill had run into the wheelhouse and was calling "Mayday, Mayday!" into our radio. I grabbed the wheel and turned *Little Mac* hard to port, moving toward the sinking plane. If there were any survivors, our big old flat barge would have plenty of room for them. "Get all the life preservers you can find!" I shouted to Bill. He collected armfuls, flinging them on deck. Then he began cleating lines to the barge and throwing the free ends into the water. The deck of the barge was only four feet above the waterline. Survivors might be able to grab hold of those lines and pull themselves aboard.

I steered the rig around the hulk of the plane, approaching it nose to nose, inching along toward the forward exit. *Careful now*, I said to myself, *don't go too far or you'll crush that plane like an eggshell.* By this time, dazed-looking people were plunging from the open doorway into the water. "Jump," one of the crew members was shouting, "you *must* jump!"

As we came closer, more and more bobbing heads appeared in the murky water. Some of the passengers could swim; others couldn't. Some had life preservers; some didn't. Some clutched seat cushions; others clung to the plane's fuselage. The water seemed to be getting rougher, and a strong current was sweeping past the plane, carrying people out into the darkness. I wondered if anyone had heard our radio call and if help was on the way.

I lost all track of time. It was like a nightmare fishing trip in which Bill and I fished for survivors. We beamed the spotlight in the direction of their cries, then urged them to climb the lines that dangled from our barge. Jet fuel had gushed out of the plane, people were soaked with it. Some of our lines were getting too slippery to handle. I knew that the tiniest spark could ignite an inferno.

By now, since the water was only thirteen feet deep, the 727 had sunk as far as it was going to go. Most of the fuselage was under water. I ran the barge over one of the submerged wings and managed to tuck *Little Mac's* flying bridge under the plane's tail assembly that rose like a silvery channel marker high out of the water. Bill was on the barge, working like a madman. At first he thought of jumping in to grab some of the people who were floundering in the sea beneath him, but he changed his mind. Instead he clamped his legs around a cleat, then leaned over the side to lift the terrified survivors in his strong arms. People straggled aboard wherever and however they could, gasping, retching, thanking God, then turning around to help somebody else. Among them I suddenly spotted a neighbor of mine, a physician who was an experienced CB operator. "Joe!" I yelled. "Get on that radio." He did, and he stayed on it, calling for help.

More time went by. There was a lot of shouting and yelling, especially from the injured trying to get our attention, but there was no panic. "Hang on! We'll get to you," the people already on board shouted. "Swim this way! We'll throw you a rope." Someone put a plank from the barge to the plane's fuselage. A few of the weak and injured were slid up onto the plane's exposed back until they could be carried across the plank. The first man I saw come across was Bill. He had two people on his back. And when at last we had fished out everybody we could find, Bill dived into the water and down into the cabin of the 727 to make sure that nobody was left inside.

Other boats finally found their way to us in the fog, bringing help to a wet and shivering collection of survivors. The main rescue work was done, though. There had been fifty-eight people aboard the plane. Three of them were drowned. I am still haunted by our failure to save them.

And yet . . .

I am also haunted by other feelings. Not a day goes by that I don't think about why I was in that particular place in the world at that particular time. I think of the barge with its ample space, its powerful spotlight, its lifelines, even the large wooden plank lying on its deck, waiting to be used. I think of my choice of Bill Kenney, and his youth, his strength, his courage. I think of my reluctance to go on that all-night voyage, and how I couldn't seem not to go. And then I think of my own personal trust in God, and how I am absolutely certain that He is aware of every move of my life.

That's when I know why I went out that foggy night into Escambia Bay, and why Somebody wanted me there.

Our Dream Cabin

— Brenda Strauch —

It was during a summer vacation that my husband, Lee, discovered a 125-year-old Lincoln log cabin atop a hill in Minnesota. It was on the verge of falling down, the logs rotted away at the foundation. But he had a dream that it could be made into a snug, warm and comfortable home. Pretty soon that dream was shared by the whole family and little by little, over our summer vacations, the cabin was rebuilt.

It was slow, hard work. But when our work was finished we had a home that represented the kind of life we longed for: simple and unhurried, with plenty of time to know God and appreciate His unspoiled creation. All around us we enjoyed acres of virtually untouched countryside; forests full of deer, badger, racoon; a lake where beavers built their homes; air that was sharp and clean. We decided to move there permanently.

It should have been deeply satisfying, but something was very wrong. Leaving California for the summers had been easy—but being out in the middle of nowhere year around, miles from city conveniences, put stresses on us I hadn't imagined.

One evening while Heather, fourteen, and Melissa, fifteen, watched TV, Eric, eighteen, read in his loftbed, and my husband, Lee, repaired our truck down at the foot of the hill. I fixed myself a hot cup of tea and took advantage of an unoccupied moment to think. But from the next room I could hear Heather's voice:

"At least in California we could get more than one channel," she said.

"Will you please stop complaining?" Melissa replied. "This is one of my favorite programs."

"Well, it's not mine!" I snapped from the other room. "Turn it down!"

The truth was, we were all getting on one another's nerves. I could understand only too well the meaning of the pioneer malady so well-named by the early settlers: "cabin fever." Just this morning I had remarked that we were down to only five gallons of water. Lee had practically jumped at me when I mentioned it to him.

"Well, I'll bring it from the Stewarts' in the truck," he said shortly, "but the kids will have to haul it up the hill whether they like it or not!"

"You bring it. They'll haul it," I replied irritably.

Hauling water wasn't exactly a chore we had bargained for. Because cold weather had set in early, we hadn't had time to get the well dug before the ground froze. In the summer it had been simple to bring water from our nearest neighbors, the Stewarts, two miles away. Now, whenever there was new snow, someone had to harness himself to the toboggan and haul twenty gallons at a time the last third of a mile.

"Cabin fever" wasn't our only problem. We also had money problems. Lee's temporary job with the Parks Department, working to clear a snowmobile path, had just ended and his jewelry business couldn't get started until spring. Our savings would just have to hold out until then.

None of these things would matter, I thought, *if we could still feel the presence of God.* It was Sunday but we hadn't gone to church—we were homesick for our old congregation back in California. We hadn't even had our own private time of praise and thanks. We no longer gathered in the evenings for Bible reading and prayer; the hymns that were always on our lips in our former home seemed to have been left behind. *Along with our Father,* I thought bleakly.

Suddenly, with one word, the nightmare began: "Fire! There's a fire up here!" Eric screamed from the loft.

I jumped up and ran into the other room. The television set went dark; the lights went out.

"What happened?" I screamed.

"I don't know. I was asleep!" (Later we found the shorted-out socket to Eric's reading lamp.)

Except for the ominous orange glow from the loft, the house was pitch black. The harsh odor of smoke began filling the air. In my frenzied mind only one thing was clear: The forty-five gallons of water we had on hand would never be enough to quench the flames. Our CB radio was on the blink;

we had no phone. "Run to the Stewarts!" I shouted to no one in particular.

Heather didn't hesitate. Taking no time to find her boots or coat, she ran out into the snowy, dark night. Later, she told me her extraordinary story.

The moon was no more than a sliver and Heather could barely make out the trees along the road. The air was like ice and as she ran she made sure to inhale only through her nose to protect her lungs, occasionally dipping her head into her sweater for a deep breath.

At the bottom of the hill she saw Lee. He looked up at her, startled. Not stopping, she cried to him. "The cabin's on fire! I'm going to the Stewarts!"

She had gone only halfway when, misjudging a bend in the road, she fell into a snowbank up to her thighs. She panicked and started to cry, "O God! O God—help me!" Frantically she struggled to climb out of the snow, but her legs felt like rubber and she couldn't feel her fingers or toes at all.

Then she heard His voice, just as clearly and simply as if any earthly person had been there. No trumpets, no heavenly choirs. Just these calm reassuring words: "I'm with you." She knew it was the Lord.

She was stunned, but she managed to gasp. "Thank You, Jesus."

Now that He was with her, Heather knew she would make it to the Stewarts. She pushed her way out of the snow and ran down the dark road as fast as she could, not caring about the numbness in her feet or the bursting feeling in her lungs.

It wasn't until she slammed open the unlocked door of the Stewarts' house and collapsed into a chair that she knew she had been running on the Lord's power alone. "Our cabin's on fire," she panted, with every bit of strength she had left.

After Heather had run for help, Melissa and I started a bucket brigade up to the loft. Melissa, who at fifteen weighs only ninety-seven pounds, would grab one of those forty-five-pound buckets and lift it over her head to me as I clung to the ladder. With my free hand I lifted them up to Eric, who was pulling flaming blankets from the burning cupboard and dousing them with water.

Isolated as we were from even a small town, I realized with a stab of fresh panic the danger we'd be in if we lost our shelter or were injured. The cabin was all we owned—without it we'd all be helpless. . . .

We all started praying then, for the moment's need, whatever it was. The smoke in the loft was becoming so thick I feared for Eric's life. "Lord, protect Eric from the smoke." I prayed. Instantly, the smoke thinned out.

I stopped my prayers of petition and began prayers of thanks and praise. "Thank You, Lord, for being with us and helping us. Thank You! Praise Your holy name!"

When Lee burst in and set to work with an axe and crowbar I prayed. "Thank You, Lord, for helping Lee break away those flaming boards off the roof!"

Not twenty minutes after Heather's brave run into the snow, the Stewarts rushed in with fire extinguishers.

"Heather's all right." Donnie Stewart said. "She's with a friend back at our place."

With their help, we sprayed foam on the remaining flames. In minutes the fire was out.

A half hour later the fire marshal arrived. Alone. "The pump truck got stuck in a ditch and our ladder truck can't get up that steep driveway of yours," he said. "You folks are lucky your house didn't burn to the ground."

"No," I murmured, "not lucky, blessed."

The Lord had looked after us in ways we could never have anticipated. If Lee had given in to his reluctance to get more water that morning we'd have had just five gallons instead of forty-five. If Eric had not been in the loft when the lamp socket shorted, the fire would have been out of control before we were even aware of it since our wood stoves fill the house with the odor of burning wood all the time. And if the Lord had not helped pull Heather out of the snow, she might not have made it.

Perhaps most remarkable of all was what Carole Stewart told me when the excitement began to die down.

"That friend of ours who's visiting, by the way, just happens to be a trained nurse."

Surely, it was more than coincidence that a nurse was visiting the Stewarts. With her immediate attention, Heather's recovery from frostbite and exposure was quick and almost painless.

Today there are a few fire marks left, adding a bit of character to the wood of the house, but the real scars are healed. The scars of doubt and desertion, of loss of sharing between members of the household and God—all were wiped away by His presence that night. We joined a church community nearby and reinstated our family worship time. Once again we feel Him close to us. We know that however far we may let ourselves stray, God is with us.

Explosion over Little Rock

— Jamie Buckingham —

The huge Strategic Air Command bomber swung into position for takeoff. The six jet engines whined with power as they lifted the giant aircraft off the runway into the gray light of dawn. Climbing slowly, since it was fully loaded with highly volatile fuel (the equivalent of three large tank truckloads), the B-47 turned on a heading that would put it over the heart of nearby Little Rock, Arkansas, in less than five minutes, at an altitude of 18,000 feet. The date was March 31, 1960.

In the copilot's seat, 1st Lt. Tom Smoak, a native of Richmond, Virginia, let his thoughts run back to the hours before takeoff. The alarm had gone off at 3:15 A.M. and he had slipped quietly out of bed to keep from waking his wife, Betsy. He followed his usual custom of spending those first few moments reading his Bible, communing with God in a "quiet time."

Tom picked up a card on which he had written a Bible verse he intended to memorize on this particular flight. It read: "The steps of a good man are ordered by the Lord: and he delighteth in his way. Though he fall, he shall not be utterly cast down: for the Lord upholdeth him with his hand" (Psalm 37:23–24).

Opening the closet he looked at the two flight suits that hung before him. One was the light, comfortable nylon suit which pilots prefer to wear. The other was the heavy, bulky, fire-resistant suit which he seldom wore because of its awkwardness. Tom reached for the heavy flight suit. He didn't question the decision, simply having a deep feeling that God intended it to be that way. The morning of miracles had begun.

The radio crackled to life in the cockpit of the B-47. Tom wrote a message on his clipboard as the plane climbed up to 18,000 feet. Suddenly it began to lurch and vibrate violently. Tom knew that the airplane was out of control and automatically reached for the ejection seat release in case he needed it. He never got a chance to pull the release. Without warning the airplane exploded. It was 6:07 A.M. and they were directly over the heart of Little Rock.

Tom's only thought was escape. The canopy blew off but before he could fire the seat ejection release he was instantaneously immersed in tons of burning fuel that poured into the cockpit. Tom knew he was going to die.

There were more explosions as the fuel tanks under the cockpit ignited. The fuselage broke in two immediately behind him. Tom screamed at the top of his lungs. He prayed. Not that he would live, but that he would die quickly. Strapped in the wreckage, he was burning alive as he hurtled towards the earth below.

Tom's helmet was ripped off by the force of the explosions. His whole head was engulfed in flames. His hands were a mass of burning flesh. The fire-resistant suit melted where it stretched tightly across his knees and shoulders.

Tom passed out from the pain. When he opened his eyes moments later his head was bent grotesquely forward and the only thing his eyes could focus on was his safety belt.

All his training warned him against loosening that belt. To loosen the belt would disengage the automatic ejection seat, his only hope of escape. Yet in that fleeting moment of consciousness, going against all training, he reached forward with a burning hand and released the safety belt. Again, he lapsed into unconsciousness.

When he opened his eyes a second time he was swinging from his parachute—free from the wreckage which was plummeting towards the city below. He assumed his ejection seat had fired anyway, or that he had released his parachute manually.

What actually had happened was that the fire which burned Tom so badly also burned away the canvas parachute pack. When Tom loosened his safety belt it separated him from his seat and allowed the parachute to unravel inside the cockpit. The wind, whistling through the falling wreckage, grabbed the parachute silk and literally sucked him out of the fuselage, allowing him to float free of the falling plane.

The pain was gone. As he dangled from the cords of his parachute he watched the wreckage plummet into the heart of the city below. Fires were breaking out in a dozen different places as the burning fuel splashed onto the innocent roofs.

Suddenly he realized the parachute was not descending at a normal rate. In fact, the ground was rushing up toward him at incredible speed. He tore his gaze away from the earth and looked upwards. The same fire that had burned off the canvas pack had also burned away one-fourth of the chute itself. He wasn't floating, but hurtling towards the housetops below. He began to pray again.

Others were praying also.

At 6:07 A.M. most of the people in the city were just getting up. Like many others, Mrs. O.B. Holeman heard the ear-shattering explosion and raced into her front yard. What she saw horrified her. Three and a half miles above the city was a tremendous fireball. Seven minutes later, out of that fireball, appeared a rapidly falling parachute. She began to pray for that lone, dangling survivor.

Her husband tried to calm her, but she became almost hysterical beseeching the Lord to save that helpless man. As she prayed, Tom Smoak's streaming parachute slipped him away from the heart of the city—directly towards the Holeman's backyard.

Mrs. Holeman, a nurse, said, "I was standing in my front yard and saw him coming down at a tremendous rate of speed, going over my rooftop, and into my back yard." She screamed as he disappeared, realizing that he would smash into her concrete driveway.

Even though Tom had led his class in basic training in parachute jumping, he knew that this time the end had come. One boot had been burned off. The horribly burned flesh was exposed. He breathed a final prayer of commitment as he saw the concrete driveway rush up to meet him.

The summer before the Holemans had debated cutting down two identical trees that spanned their driveway. They decided to let them stand. That morning, when Tom Smoak hurtled out of the heavens, his streaming parachute snagged the tops of both trees. They were the exact height of the combined length of his parachute silk, cords, and his body. As he flashed by them they grabbed his chute, bent inward just enough to let him recline softly on the driveway, and then gently straightened up, pulling him into an upright position.

When the Holemans and their neighbors rushed into the back yard, instead of a broken body they found a badly burned but very much alive Tom Smoak, standing on his good foot—and giving orders how to unfasten the parachute harness.

Two persons died on the ground that morning, and of the four crewmen aboard the plane Tom Smoak was the only survivor.

Tom spent the next two years going through twenty operations for plastic surgery. The doctors marveled that no fire had touched his lungs, eyes, or throat.

Because Tom Smoak believes that God saves to serve, today [written in 1968] he is back in the air again. This time he flies for the Lord as a member of the flying team for Wycliffe Bible Translators. He knows that a day committed to God is never wasted. And occasionally as he pilots missionaries and Bible translators into the steaming jungles of South

America, Tom remembers that morning of miracles and he likes to paraphrase a verse that explains for him the whole experience of that day: "For he shall give his angels charge over thee, to keep thee in all thy ways. They shall bear thee up in their hands, lest thou dash thy foot against" a concrete driveway—(Psalm 91:11–12).

Against All Odds

— Cheryl Deep —

I stared at our seven-month-old baby girl, Chelsea, in the hospital crib. As I tucked up her blanket, my eyes rested on the old Dillon family Bible I kept in the crib with her. It had belonged to my grandmother, who died when I was thirteen. I cherished that Bible as I had cherished my grandmother. She always soothed my childhood hurts and fears; to this day I still missed her. The Bible had rested in her hands during her funeral service. My mother removed it just before the coffin lid was lowered, and later gave it to me.

But even Grandmother probably could not have soothed the hurt and fear my husband, Lance, and I now faced. Earlier that day the specialists at University Medical Center in Tucson had finally diagnosed the baffling condition that was slowly but surely draining the life from our first child.

"Chelsea has an extremely rare birth defect called severe combined immunodeficiency syndrome," our doctor informed us. "SCIDS interferes with the normal functioning of her immune system. She has virtually no natural defenses against infection. Her bone marrow doesn't produce the necessary cells."

I stood statue-still and stared at him. I remembered the movie *Boy in the Plastic Bubble* about a child with the same condition. All along we'd hoped it was some obscure but defeatable bug causing the fever, diarrhea and weight loss that ravaged Chelsea. I had prayed that somewhere in the mighty arsenal of modern medicine was the right drug, the magic bullet that would cure her. The immunologist carefully explained that the only option was a bone marrow transplant—a risky procedure that at best had about a fifty percent chance of success.

The *only* option.

We needed to transfer her to a hospital that did this sort of operation as soon as possible, he had said. There were only a few in the entire country.

Now as I stood over Chelsea's crib I smoothed the blanket and pushed the old Bible off to the side. Its leather cover was worn soft with use. As my child slept I closed my eyes and hoped for a miracle.

The next day we decided on Memorial Sloan-Kettering in Manhattan for the procedure because of their slightly-higher-than-average success rate. But now came the enormous problem of transporting Chelsea from Tucson to New York without exposing her to many people. Chelsea couldn't afford to catch even a cold. Any worsening in her condition would delay surgery. A simple flu bug could kill her.

Driving there was out of the question. She couldn't be off

her IV fluids for that long. Commercial airliners posed too much hazard of contracting contagious disease, and big airports were even worse. We needed a private plane, but Chelsea's condition was not considered acutely critical, a criterion that had to be met before our insurance company would agree to cover the enormous cost of a jet. The catch-22 was that if Chelsea did become that critical, she would probably be too sick to have the surgery.

Lance and I were at wit's end. We didn't sleep, we barely ate. There had to be something we could do. We made countless phone calls. Finally we heard about a group called Corporate Angels, which provides free flights for sick children aboard private planes. The flights conduct normal business travel and patients hitch along. Corporate Angels found us a flight leaving that Friday out of Denver bound nonstop for New York. A miracle was in our grasp.

"Dear God," I prayed, "now please help us get to Denver. I know You have Your ways. We'll just keep on trying."

Denver was too far to drive. We got the number of a private medivac company. Maybe we could pay for the flight ourselves. But when I talked to Judy Barrie, a paramedic whose husband, Jim, piloted the medivac plane, she gave me the bad news: "The flight will cost six thousand dollars, minimum," she said. We didn't have $6,000. Our finances had been stretched to the limit.

I thanked Judy and said good-bye. "Wait," she said suddenly as I was about to hang up, "I really want to help you. I'm not promising anything, but I'll talk to Jim. Maybe he can figure this out."

When I hung up I had the strangest feeling that these people would be able to do something about what was increasingly a hopeless situation. An hour later Jim Barrie called back. "Listen, I've got a friend deadheading from Phoenix to Denver in the morning," Jim told me. (Deadheading meant he was flying back an empty plane.) "If you can get to the field by six-thirty, you can hitch along."

Perfect. Chelsea could handle the drive to Phoenix. But I was almost afraid to ask the next question. "Jim, what will it cost?"

"Cost? Heck, not a thing. This guy's a friend, and he's got to get his plane up there anyway."

I was faint with relief. These total strangers had taken a huge step in saving the life of my child. I didn't know what to say. The word *thanks* didn't seem big enough.

"You could do us one little favor, though," Jim added. "Judy and I would like to meet Chelsea."

Chelsea was awake and even a bit playful when Jim and Judy arrived at the hospital. While Jim talked to Lance about finding our way around the Phoenix airport, Judy and I chatted. Her eyes kept flitting over to the crib. Then I noticed she was staring at Grandma's Bible. One time when Judy was leaning over Chelsea, her fingers brushed it. Finally, as they were about to go, Judy asked, "Where are you from?" I told her Pittsburgh.

"I'm from Pittsburgh too," she said slowly. "Well, Carnegie actually."

"My mother is from Carnegie," I said. I felt a shiver go through me. "Virginia Everett. Dillon was her maiden name."

"Virginia Dillon?" Judy said, eyes wide. "My father was Howard Dillon."

"Uncle Howard?" I was stunned.

Judy nodded. It was as if a current of electricity had jumped between us. Now I could see why her face had seemed faintly familiar. Judy Barrie was my cousin Judy Dillon. "I haven't seen you since . . ." I started to say. Judy's eyes jumped again to the Bible.

"Since Grandma's funeral twenty years ago," she finished the sentence. "That's the Bible she was holding."

We fell into each other's arms. I knew then that all would be well with Chelsea. The odds against this crossing of paths were simply too great. This was meant to be.

Chelsea got her bone marrow transplant and four months later she left the hospital with a healthy immune system. She is, as they say, a medical miracle.

And then there was that other miracle. I like to think of it as my grandmother's miracle. In a sense, even twenty years after her funeral, she was reaching out to comfort me and to assure me that with God all things are possible.

A NOTE FROM
THE EDITORS

Angels, Miracles, and Messages, was created by the book division of the company that publishes *Guideposts,* a monthly magazine filled with true stories of people's adventures in faith.

Guideposts magazine is not sold on the newsstand. It's available by subscription only. And subscribing is easy. All you have to do is write to Guideposts, 39 Seminary Hill Road, Carmel, New York 10512.

When you subscribe, each month you can count on receiving exciting new evidence of God's presence, His guidance and His limitless love for all of us.